Folk Music and Modern Sound

Folk Music and Modern Sound

EDITED BY
William Ferris and Mary L. Hart

UNIVERSITY PRESS OF MISSISSIPPI
JACKSON

Center for the Study of Southern Culture Series

Copyright ᶜ 1982 by the University Press of Mississippi
All Rights Reserved
Manufactured in the United States of America

Print-on-Demand Edition.

Publication of this book was made possible in part by a grant from the Andrew W. Mellon Foundation

Library of Congress Cataloging in Publication Data

Main entry under title:
Folk music and modern sound.
   Based on lectures presented at a conference at the University of Mississippi, Apr. 17-19, 1980.
   Includes index.
   1. Folk music—History and criticism. I. Ferris, William R. II. Hart, Mary L.
ML3545.F63   784.4'973   82-2041
ISBN: 978-1-60473-167-5   AACR2

Contents

Introduction *William Ferris* vii

The Anglo Connection
The Impact of Recording Technology on the British
  Folksong Revival *Kenneth S. Goldstein* 3
Electric Folk Music in Britain *A.L. Lloyd* 14

Ethnic Voices
How the Fiddler Got on the Roof *Mark Slobin* .. 21
Slovenian Style in Milwaukee *Charles Keil* 32
Ethnic and Popular Style in America
  Richard Spottswood 60

The Religious Sound
New Directions in Sacred Harp Singing
  Doris J. Dyen 73
Gospel Goes Uptown: White Gospel Music, 1945-1955
  Charles K. Wolfe 80
The Secularization of Black Gospel Music
  Anthony Heilbut 101

Pure Country
Honky Tonk: The Music of the Southern Working Class
   Bill C. Malone 119
Commercialization and Tradition in the Nashville
   Sound   *William Ivey* 129

Myths and Heroes
Charles Ives: Victorian Gentleman or American Folk
   Hero? *Vivian Perlis* 141
Myths About Black Folk Music *Dena J. Epstein* . 151

Blacks and Blues
Blues and Modern Sound: Past, Present, and Future
   David Evans 163
Black Music: Its Roots, Its Popularity, Its Commercial
   Prostitution *Amiri Baraka* 177
Folk, Popular, Jazz, and Classical Elements in New
   Orleans *Robert Palmer* 194
Contributors 202
Index 205

INTRODUCTION

The collection, study, and commercialization of American folksong in this century is a rich and varied tale. The folksong movement has roots in the romantic transcendentalist emphasis on return to nature and the common man as expressed in Thoreau's philosophy. Whitman's poetry in turn identifies the common man as the source of America's spirit. His "I Hear America Singing" in *Leaves of Grass* (1855) is then echoed in Carl Sandburg's *American Songbag* (1927) and *The People Yes* (1936).

The love of Whitman and Sandburg for folk music was shared by dedicated fieldworkers such as John and Alan Lomax, who amassed large folksong collections, many of which are deposited in the Library of Congress Archive of Folk Song. Established in 1928, the Archive attracted a distinguished list of scholars who directed its efforts to collect and study folksong. These scholars edited over sixty long-playing records featuring Native American, Afro-, Anglo-, and ethnic American folk musics. Using collections in the Archive as a base for research, ethnomusicologist Charles Seeger explored connections between music and class structure in the United States. In his study of "Cantometrics" Alan Lomax showed links between folksong style and American culture in a methodology that he later applied to culture zones throughout the world. In this study Lomax used a computer to correlate large bodies of data and in his similar "Choreometrics" study he later showed links between dance style and culture.

While fieldworkers like Lomax gathered and studied folksongs, the record industry issued thousands of commerical folk recordings, many of which date from the beginning of this century. Afro-American "race," white "hillbilly," and ethnic commercial recordings are an important compliment to folksong archives such as that in the Library of Congress. Many of these commercial issues were recorded by field units of companies like RCA that travelled to remote areas in search of undiscovered performers. The result was a rich harvest that included musicians such as Jimmie Rodgers, the Father of Country Music.

An important link developed between the folksong movement and social change as labor and Civil Rights leaders repeatedly turned to folk music to state their causes. In the 1940s folk singers like Leadbelly, Aunt Molly Jackson, and Woody Guthrie drew widespread support through their music and influenced young white musicians such as Pete Seeger and Bess Lomax Hawes who sang with the Weavers and the Almanac Singers. Their music was chronicled by *Sing Out!* magazine and appeared on numerous Folkways recordings issued by Moses Asch. During the 1960s the Civil Rights movement mobilized group support with "We Shall Overcome," and gifted black vocalists such as Bernice Reagan organized the Student Nonviolent Coordinating Committee's Freedom Singers in support of the movement. The folk music revival of the sixties also established a commercial market for protest folksingers such as Joan Baez and Bob Dylan. As Americans sought to rediscover musical roots, the Newport and Smithsonian Folklife Festivals became national celebrations of folksong. These and smaller regional festivals continue to be an important public platform for American folk music.

Recent discographies, studies of the recording industry, and large record collections now make commercial recordings a major resource for folksong study. Important archives of these recordings exist at the Country Music Foundation in Nashville, the Tulane Jazz Archives in New Orleans, the John Edwards Memorial Foundation in Los Angeles, and the YIVO Institute for Jewish Research in New York. Like the Library of Congress Archive of Folk Song, each has sponsored important fieldwork and has issued books and records on folksong.

The 1970s saw the creation of the long-awaited Library of Congress American Folklife Center. Using teams of folklorists the Center launched important regional projects in Georgia, Chicago, and Montana, and established important links with Departments such as Interior and Agriculture. Also during the seventies, the National Endowment for the Arts Folk Arts Panel and the National Endowment for the Humanities Special Projects Division provided important support for folk musicians, festivals, and scholarship.

Folk music scholarship, institutional archives, and federal support of research in this country are enriched by a distinguished body of European research on American folk music. Shortly after World War I a jazz appreciation movement began in Europe, and for several decades the systematic collection of jazz records and the publication of works and periodicals devoted to the music took place almost exclusively in Europe. While Alfons Dauer's *Der Jazz* (1958) analyzed African polyphony and rhythms in jazz, in England Paul Oliver shaped blues scholarship through *Blues Fell This Morning* (1960), *Screening the Blues* (1968), and *The Story of the Blues* (1969). The Institut für Jazzforschung in Graz, Austria, and the *Folk Music Year Book* in England reflect a continuing European interest in American folk music.

From the perspective of the eighties, important questions about contemporary folk music are being raised. The process through which traditional folk music assumes new forms is complex, a tangle of effects by such forces as urbanization, industrialization, migration, new technology, and, particularly in the United States, the invigorating mix of cultures from many lands. Equally complex—but perhaps more hotly debated—is the question of what this transformation means for the continuity of traditional music itself.

To seek answers to such questions the University of Mississippi sponsored a conference on "Folk Music and Modern Sound" from April 17 through April 19, 1980, which brought together scholars and writers from fields of folklore, ethnomusicology, history, music criticism, poetry, anthropology, and music bibliography. Many of the speakers exchanged ideas at the conference for the first time. The essays in this volume are based on lectures originally presented at that conference and reflect both the challenge and the fascination of the search.

The first section, "The Anglo Connection," studies the impact of technology on folk music in general and on the British folksong revival in particular. Kenneth Goldstein concentrates on the importance of the tape recorder and long-playing record in the revival that began in Britain in the early 1950s and continues today. These two products of technical advance, he writes, are only the latest in the long line of communications improvements that began with the invention of movable type in the fifteenth century. Each has subsequently helped to produce a folksong revival. But far from changing the nature of folksong itself, as is often charged, Goldstein finds that each successive communications revolution has "supplemented rather than replaced, reinforced rather than displaced, fed rather than swallowed, the oral tradition." A.L. Lloyd then traces the rise in the 1960s of "the tendency to transport folksong lock, stock, and barrel into the world of electronics." Changes in the style and presentation of folksong, such as this use of amplification, are often greeted with dismay by those concerned with authenticity. However, Lloyd observes, such innovation is not new. Folk music has a history of change based upon technological, cultural, and social change—"otherwise in the Anglo-Saxon world we'd still be singing melodies based on a 3-note scale and banging a couple of sticks together as an accompaniment."

Introduction

Ethnomusicologist Mark Slobin, in the section on "Ethnic Voices," delineates New York's internal Jewish-American popular music world early in this century. Closely linked to the Yiddish-American theater, it very early exhibited two important trends—toward eclecticism and toward increasing Americanization. Slobin shows that it was the intersection of the music of this world with the music of Broadway that made possible—indeed, probable—a musical such as the internationally acclaimed *Fiddler on the Roof*. Charles Keil, drawing on recorded interviews, then pursues the mystery of the missing Polish polka bands in Milwaukee—a polka center having half a million Poles as its largest ethnic group but a decided preference for Slovenian-style polka, as typified in the polka music of Frankie Yankovic. Finally, Richard Spottswood, editor of the Library of Congress's recorded series Folk Music in America, surveys commercial ethnic recording in the United States since the early 1900s. Noting that little attention has been paid to the place of ethnic music in the development of America's music, he urges that a new emphasis be placed on the study and collecting of ethnic recordings since they "seem today to be the only meaningful access to this music of the past."

Doris Dyen, leading off the section on "The Religious Sound," looks at the relationship of Sacred Harp singing to two groups of outsiders: the mass media and the scholars and fieldworkers who document the tradition. Using as a microcosm the black concert ensemble Wiregrass Sacred Harp Singers, she shows that both groups of outsiders "by their very efforts to document a tradition, assume an active role in encouraging and even initiating changes in that tradition." Charles Wolfe follows with an analysis of the commercialization in the forties and fifties of white gospel music. In 1948, with its recording "Gospel Boogie," the Homeland Harmony Quartet of Atlanta became history's first Southern white gospel group to have a hit record. Wolfe identifies and elaborates on four influences in the postwar gospel world that made it possible for such quartets to become professionals, thus breaking away from the singing conventions from which they sprang. In his paper on black gospel music, Anthony Heilbut also explores the theme of commercialization. Concentrating on the period from 1940 to 1960—"Gospel's Golden Age"—he isolates and explains the elements that fostered a convergence of the religious and the secular in songs and styles of such performers as Sister Rosetta Tharpe. He then concludes with a survey of the continuing strong influence of black gospel on American popular music.

In the section "Pure Country," Bill Malone focuses on the years during and after World War II "when the music of the honky tonk became, at least for a time, virtually *the* sound of country music." Malone shows that, as rural white Southerners moved to urban centers, this music increasingly reflected their tensions and concerns. Hank Williams, the greatest honky tonk singer of them all, Malone writes, "sang to an audience, who, for better or worse, were having to come to terms with life in an industrial-urban environment." William Ivey follows with a discussion of the relationship of early country music to the modern "Nashville Sound." Noting the hostility of many scholars to popular or commercial elements as destructive to folk music, Ivey argues that, on the contrary, the music produced in Nashville's studios from 1957 to 1971 "can be viewed as a very positive step in the accommodation between commercial sophistication and primitive traditional art."

Vivian Perlis opens the section on "Myths and Heroes" by examining the paradoxes that abound in the life and music of Charles Ives. A gentleman of impeccable upper-class Victorian background, Ives, nevertheless, holds solid credentials as "folk hero." However, as Perlis shows, it is his political and social ideas, rather than the extensive use of folk material in his music, that place him in "a unique position among 'serious' composers as a man of the people." Dena Epstein follows with a study of the myth that black spirituals were wholly derived from white spirituals. Early collectors of this music, she shows, working before the wide availability of recording

Introduction xiii

equipment, were forced to transcribe what they heard into standard musical notation. Because this system "filtered out all non-European stylistic elements" black performance style "now regarded as supremely important, was ignored."

In the final section, "Blacks and Blues," David Evans considers the blues, past, present, and future. Observing that this music has had "the peculiar reputation of being something both primitive and modern," he surveys the extensive contributions that blues has made to almost every major American musical style and form in this century. "Yet the blues remains a distinct musical form with its own traditions," Evans writes. For the future, he predicts that a renewal of interest in this music that he detects among young black people will be a sustaining force for the blues. Amiri Baraka shares Evans's belief that Afro-American music frames much of America's popular music and reminds us that the music bears both the memory of Africa and the reality of Afro-American slavery. He traces the history and influence of black music from the blues, born after the Civil War "of the versifier, the magician, in motion through the South," through jazz to today's "perversion of the blues impulse and form" in disco. Throughout he elaborates on his belief that in the United States "black music is viewed as raw material to be wrung dry" by the white entertainment and recording industries and that "the black innovator . . . is swallowed." In the final paper Robert Palmer shows that early rock and roll of the fifties coming from cities such as Chicago, Los Angeles, Memphis, and New Orleans had distinctive regional characteristics. Both the musical and social history of an area played a "crucial role . . . the richer an area's musical traditions the richer the rock and roll produced there." For this reason he focuses on rock and roll in New Orleans during the period and "the dialectic between folk, popular, jazz, and classical elements one finds there."

Speakers stressed that folk music reflects contemporary experience. As Polish polka and Yiddish folksong performers moved from rural life in Eastern Europe to urban centers in the United States, black blues and white country singers in this country also shifted from rural to urban worlds, and cities like New York, Milwaukee, Chicago, Nashville, Memphis, and New Orleans had a major influence on their music. Singers with divergent racial, ethnic, and linguistic histories adapted traditional music forms to new, often threatening worlds, and their songs trace European and Southern ethnic diasporas within the United States. As each contributor explores traditional and modern forms, each shows how performers shape music in a variety of racial and ethnic traditions. Together they merge blues, country, Yiddish, Polish, and Sacred Harp singers in an Ives-like tribute to folk music and modern sound.

Throughout the conference concerts by traditional folk musicians from the region and video-tapes on Delta blues, jazz, gospel, ballads, and country music were mixed with formal papers. Three evening performances before large, enthusiastic audiences highlighted major topics discussed at the conference. Bill Mitchell, a national champion old-time fiddler, was introduced by Alan Jabbour, Director of the American Folklife Center at the Library of Congress, who gave a summary of country fiddle tunes in America. John Arnold and the Duck Hillbillies presented bluegrass music after an introduction by Ralph Rinzler, Director of the Folklife Program at the Smithsonian Institution. And I introduced the blues performance that began with Memphis vocalist Sid Selvidge on piano accompanied by *New York Times* critic Robert Palmer on clarinet. The program concluded with James "Son" Thomas performing Mississippi Delta blues.

Special thanks are due to the Mississippi Committee for the Humanities and the Mississippi Folklore Society for their support, and to Jerry Speir and Keith Sharon who coordinated the program. Excellent evaluations of the conference were provided by Gilbert Chase, Jeff Titon, and Berndt Ostendorf.

William Ferris
University of Mississippi, Oxford, Mississippi

PART I

The Anglo Connection

The Impact of Recording Technology on the British Folksong Revival

Kenneth S. Goldstein

THE FOLKSONG REVIVAL in Britain, begun after World War II and continuing to the present, is a complex phenomenon. It is not an easy task to unravel the many strands which make up the warp and woof of its fabric. The few such attempts, including *The Electric Muse* with important contributions on the British scene by Karl Dallas and Robin Denselow,[1] and the more recent *Folk Revival: The Rediscovery of a National Music* by Fred Woods,[2] have been, at best, only partially successful in describing the phenomenon and even less so in explaining it.

It is not my intention in this short paper to either describe or explain it. Instead, I will focus on one element in an attempt to elucidate its role in the complex dynamic of process, actors, and society which makes up the folk revival. Without downgrading the real importance of social and intellectual history, aesthetics, economics, politics, and personalities in the development of the folk revival, I intend to concentrate on the importance of the tape recorder and the long-playing phonograph recording as major technological developments without which the revival could not have taken place nor lasted as long as it has.

The position I take here is essentially a "technological deterministic" one. At a conference in 1979, I first presented the hypothesis that each major technological advance in mass communication media helped to produce a folksong revival: in the fifteenth, sixteenth, and seventeenth centuries, the introduction of movable type and metal engravings resulted in a revival to which the printing of broadsides, chapbooks, and songsters contributed greatly. Offset and gravure printing, invented a couple of centuries later, contributed to another folksong revival; the invention of the sound recording machine, and later the disc phonograph record, each produced major folksong revivals; the widespread use of inexpensive radios produced still another revival and reinforced and continued the impetus of the phonographically inspired revival. Nor is the end in sight with the introduction of the tape recorder and long-playing records in the 1950s and 1960s; still standing by but ready momentarily to take its proper place in the succession of technological advances contributing to the present folksong revival is the video tape recorder, needing only a reduction in bulk and price to insure its position.

It is important to note here that each successive technological advance produced media which improved upon the communication potential of its predecessors while not replacing them. In a sense, as pointed out by D. K. Wilgus and others, the phonograph record is a direct descendent of the broadside which, however, continues to live on in sheet music, song books, and song folios. Note, too, that my position is diametrically opposed to the oft repeated one that the printing and recording of folksong freezes its form and content so that it ceases to be folksong. I believe, instead, that each successive communication revolution has speeded up its circulation through space and time. Nor have frozen texts and tunes resulted from such use of mass communication channels. They have supplemented rather than replaced, reinforced rather than displaced, fed rather than swallowed, the oral tradition.

* * *

Impact of Technology on British Folksong

Some historians of the British folksong revival trace its beginnings to Lonnie Donegan, who, in 1954, formed a group that played skiffle versions of American folksongs and blues. But as Karl Dallas points out in *The Electric Muse*, the actual roots of Donegan's skiffle lie in the "Ballads and Blues" radio programs on BBC begun in 1951 by Ewan MacColl, A. L. Lloyd, and Alan Lomax. In the mid-fifties, too, another radio program, "As I Roved Out," played field recordings of the few traditional singers known to be alive at the time. Folk clubs had come into existence in the early 1950s, and by 1956 were on their way to being a well established feature of the folk scene. Many of the clubs took rather strong stands on the musics performed in them. There were traditionalist clubs, purer than any scholar would dare to be; the blues clubs that featured American music and skiffle; and other clubs that were eclectic and encouraged the singing and performing of a full gamut of British, American, and international folk music. In 1953, Ewan MacColl opened the Ballad and Blues Club, as eclectic as its name. He later formed the Singers' Club and became the spokesman for an intense cultural chauvinism on the folk club scene. In the British revival that he espoused, singers would be permitted to perform songs only from their own culture, and especially had to avoid American songs.

Where was the repertoire of British songs to come from in this British folksong revival? The largest source would be the bowdlerized and frequently over-edited English folksong collections of the Reverend Sabine Baring-Gould, Lucy Broadwood, Cecil Sharp, Frank Kidson, and other late nineteenth- and early twentieth-century collectors. Just as these songs had eventually bored the school children and educators of an earlier folksong revival on whom they had been forced, so, too, the continual repetition of these same songs took its toll of singers and audiences of the new revival. New sources for repertoire had to be found. These could have been newly composed songs, but nobody was yet ready to call these folksongs. What was needed was newly discovered old songs. The radio program "As I Roved Out" had pointed the way to living "source" singers, and when Peter Kennedy went on a BBC-sponsored field trip with a tape recorder to discover if there were other traditional singers than the half-dozen known to him, he and his regional collaborators (especially Hamish Henderson and Seamus Ennis) found dozens more throughout England, Scotland, and Ireland. Here, then, was the new repertoire for the British folksong revival, waiting to be harvested from the crop of recently discovered traditional singers.

The magnetic tape recorder, which had been invented before the Second World War in Germany and introduced in the rest of Europe after the war, made it possible to record numerous songs in the singers' repertoires on high fidelity equipment that was considerably lighter, more compact, and easier to handle than the field disc cutters employed earlier. At almost the same time as the reinvention of the tape recorder, the long-playing phonograph record came into existence. Now the tools existed, not only for the recording of the much needed new repertoire of the burgeoning revival, but also for the issuance of those recordings in a compact and relatively inexpensive form. Instead of being heard only on radio programs, performances could be copied on tape recorders from those programs or could be issued on records. The would-be folksinger could then learn songs at leisure through repeated playbacks of the tapes or records. No longer did singers have to be able to read, and trust, the published transcriptions of early collectors. While it did not supply "instant repertoire," it produced a ready supply of good songs—good British songs at that—which could be increased as long as there were collectors, singers from whom the songs could be collected, and record companies that could and would issue the recordings. The records were first issued by small specialty houses like Topic Records and Collector Records or by private individuals. Later, HMV, Columbia, and other major producers could be persuaded to issue these records when they discovered there was a larger market for them than they had earlier imagined. The British folksong revival was alive and kicking and could look forward to a long life.

The thumbnail sketch of the first decade of the British folksong revival just recited is a quick and perhaps simplistic overview of the very complex series of phenomena referred to before; it will, however, serve to introduce the specific contributions made by the tape and long-playing recordings of traditional British and Irish singers issued during the past thirty years. It will also indicate the manner in which the new technology that produced these recordings served to supplement or improve on the kinds and amounts of cultural information communicated by earlier technology and media.

The primary result of the technological breakthroughs of the past, culminating in the recent introduction of tape recorders and long-playing records, has been to supply new media for the presentation and communication of ideas and information. From the advent of printing to the present, a not inconsiderable portion of that new information consisted of song materials. These served to supply new items for the repertoires of communities and individuals who needed them. Some of the earlier media, however, had a serious shortcoming, that of length. Only relatively short pieces could be printed on broadsides; chapbooks and songsters could present longer texts, however. Analogous to these differences are the sound recordings of the twentieth century. Seventy-eight RPM records permitted playing performances of from two-and-a-half to twelve minutes; the tape recorder could record selections of almost any length and the long-playing record is able to present performances running up to sixty minutes, more than enough time for several long ballads.

In addition to supplying new repertoire, the printed or recorded song media also helped to revive older songs and ballads lost or forgotten wholly or in part by supplying more complete texts than the fragments existing in the repertoires of some singers, thereby keeping these songs alive in tradition for an additional period of time. The songs also served as models for the inspiration of song writers. Included among pieces conceived in this manner were parodies of existing songs, answers to songs on whose subject matter there were several points of view, and entirely original pieces inspired either by the form or theme of already existing items.

We are reminded by B. H. Bronson and others that songs and ballads are more than texts. In ideal presentation, the melodies to which the words are sung should be included. Broadsides and other early printed media published only texts, though some supplied the title of the tune to which the songs could be sung. But even with the invention of movable music type, and still later with the invention of engraved music plates, only a relatively small number of published songs included music. The problem was not whether the music was included with the text but, that even if it was included, who would be able to read it? Now, as then, musical illiteracy is many times greater than textual illiteracy. As recently as 1974, when I conducted an informal survey among British revivalists, I found that fewer than thirty percent could read music. Sound recordings, however, have made musical illiteracy a moot problem. On the recording, as in life, words and tune are performed simultaneously, and the would-be singer listening to a recorded performance learns both. In the heyday of broadsides, a singer could set a text to the suggested tune, when it was indicated and if he knew it, or he could sing the text to any tune he knew whose metric line and length were appropriate. Perhaps songs were sung to a greater variety of tunes in the past. Even today, however, many songs and ballads appear in numerous versions on recordings, with the tunes as well as the texts differing, sometimes considerably, from one to another. What has happened is that more people can and have learned more songs than ever before because no special skills are needed to learn from sound recordings.

Then, too, rather than fixing tune repertoires, recordings have made it possible to select appropriate tunes from a growing melody bank. Texts usually found attached to a particular tune can be sung to one that is more to the singer's taste. One need only read the liner notes on records issued by revival singers to see how frequently texts have been learned from one source and tunes from another.

The increasingly larger melody bank has also resulted in more "new" tunes being composed. Drawing strands from a wide variety of tune models, new melodies are fabricated, usually with the singer- and instrumentalist-composers uncertain of the sources from which their musical ideas have been drawn.

Whereas texts and tunes could be obtained from either printed or sound media, though in quite different ways and requiring substantially different skills, the choice of medium does not exist when it comes to learning performance skills. Though music and text can be transcribed to the written or printed page, reasonably representing what has been sung, performance style is less amenable to such transcription. The subtle use of dynamics, timbre, and tempo changes, so critical in distinguishing European traditional singing from popular and art singing styles, is only minimally capable of being transferred to the printed page, and then usually requiring still more sophisticated transcription which further limits the audience for interpretation of the encoded information. When it comes to understanding and learning performance style, there is no real substitute for live performance or sound recordings of it.

The singer learns about style by listening to and imitating what he hears. Recordings may serve as style models, and the revival singer may choose to imitate or adopt the singing style of his favorite singer, to combine several styles, or to create a new and idiosyncratic style of his own, based on the models he has absorbed. British traditional singers like Harry Cox, Phil Tanner, Sam Larner, Jeannie Robertson, and more recently Fred Jordon, Walter Pardon, and Belle Stewart, have served as models for innumerable revival singers. The delightful glee style of singing, borrowed from the Copper family with variations by the Young Tradition and the Watersons, has affected numerous imitators of all three groups. Indeed, tape and phonographic recordings have made it possible for revival singers to learn both from traditional singers and from their more famous imitators, but without limiting the number of styles to just those favorites because of the great number of models available. In earlier days, singers learned the singing style of their relatives and neighbors through a slow socialization process. Modern day sound recordings, distributed nationally and even internationally, provide to huge immediate and potential audiences a broad array of styles and substyles on which to model their own performances. Though it may be argued that such wide distribution could result in the dissolution of the many individual and regional singing styles and their replacement by only a few styles, this has not been the case. The number of substyles within the general traditional stylistic framework has remained consistently large, and it can be shown convincingly, I believe, that homogeneity has not taken place.

To be sure, the process of learning singing style can go beyond sound recordings. Sound movies and video tape recorders have made it possible for revival singers to both hear and *see* their singing style models. Here paralinguistic and paramusical communication can be observed along with the kinesic and proxemic behaviors that contribute to what we call singing style. Indeed, as such media are further developed and produced at more reasonable prices, we can expect that traditional styles can be maintained at vital levels considerably longer than was previously possible. In the past, new styles and modes of expression regularly displaced existing ones according to changing aesthetics and fads. Older traditional styles will now permanently be available for study—and imitation—and future revivals may include styles popular at various periods in the development of a people's music.

Impact of Technology on British Folksong 11

The contribution to the present folk music revival made by tape recorders and long-playing records does not stop with the communication of texts, tunes, and performance styles, however. The issuance of long-playing recordings and tapes of traditional singers, together with their appearance at folk festivals, folk clubs, and folksong concerts, has inspired the search for and the tape recording of old singers by folksong revivalists in their own and nearby communities. Such amateur fieldwork has resulted not only in the discovery of previously unknown traditional singers, but has also resulted in the revivalist-collector feeling more secure in his own involvment with tradition. The collector usually becomes a self-conscious student of the tradition and a more responsible and understanding performer and stylist in the revival.

Revival singer-collectors sometimes bring their informant friends to festivals where such singers are appreciated and where they serve as models for attendant revivalists. Audience members usually cherish meeting old-timers, and may take advantage of the contact to indulge in name-dropping at home. I heard one folksong revivalist introduce a song at his local folk club with "I learned this song from Walter Pardon, who sang it at Loughborough." The impression given by that statement was that Walter Pardon taught him the song at the Loughborough Festival. In fact, however, while it was true that Pardon had sung at the festival, my friend had learned the song from one of his recordings. Such deception is quite innocent and merely reflects the admiration many revivalists have for the tradition and its living bearers.

The tape recordings of traditional singers made by amateur collectors on semiprofessional machines may be offered to record companies for issuance on long-playing records or tapes. Field recordings may also be presented to those companies as audition tapes, with an interested company later sending its own engineer to do the final recordings or inviting the singer to record in a studio. The matter has come full circle: long-playing recordings of traditional singers have inspired revivalists to record such singers in their own communities and to arrange for them to be issued on long-playing records for the edification and entertainment of other revivalists.

Contact with tradition through commercially issued field recordings has resulted not only in revival singers becoming better informed about folksong, but has resulted in some of them returning to school to obtain academic training in folk cultural studies. Tony Green at the University of Leeds and Dr. Robert Thompson, now teaching folklore at the University of Florida, come to mind as British academics who had their introduction to folksong through the British revival. Others with folk cultural training include revival performers like Bob Pegg and Cyril Tawney.

By way of closing this discussion I wish to mention another value of the revival to the academic folksong and ballad community, made possible by the technology referred to in this paper. Academics and revivalists have rarely been close to each other. Only a few individuals could be said to be members of both communities. The tape recorder made it possible for an increasing number of amateur collectors to do the fieldwork which previously was the domain of a few professionals. Out of this ferment of fieldwork, originally designed to serve and inform the folksong revival, has come important recorded collections which simultaneously serve as primary resource materials for academic study. Indeed, the long-playing record with its accompanying booklet of biographical notes, photographs, texts, and bibliographical, discographical, and comparative references, has become the *major* source of primary data for scholarly study. The data previously represented in journals by articles containing texts and tunes collected in the field by academic scholar-collectors has been replaced, in many cases, by commercially issued folksong recordings of traditional singers, prepared by revivalist-collectors. Such recordings, in fact, are more reliable documents than the more conventional printed ones, for they consist of objective data capable of examination and reexamination not only by the collector but by others as well. They may be subjected to various and changing interpretations in the course of analysis but they remain constant as objective reports of facts existing at the time of the recording. The same can not be said of published texts and tunes, for their transcriptions are interpretations of what the transcriber *thought* he heard and as such are not facts.

The technology which made it possible for folksong revivalists and specialty record companies to document tradition in terms of their own needs was also available to folksong scholars for their purposes. That it has not been used as frequently or as effectively by the scholars is a comment on the state of academic folksong studies in Britain. Fortunately, the scale has been more than balanced by the folksong revivalists whose contributions to such study will long be applauded and of considerable use to future generations of ballad and folksong scholars.

---

[1] Dave Laing, Robin Denselow, Karl Dallas, and Robert Shelton, *The Electric Muse* (London: Methuen, Ltd., 1975).

[2] Fred Woods, *Folk Revival: The Rediscovery of a National Music* (Poole, England: Blandford Press, 1979).

Electric Folk Music in Britian

A. L. Lloyd

FROM NATCHEZ to New Guinea, all over the world, it seems to be the destiny of folksong to be changing from a domestic and ceremonial music for insiders into a public performance music for an audience including outsiders, perhaps comprised entirely of outsiders. Technological change means changes in society, and that means changes in culture, too, including folksong. So the function of folksong alters; some bits become redundant and get lost, especially the ceremonial songs and those accompanying obsolescent work processes. Other bits assume a dominance they didn't have before, especially the shorter lyrical songs, love songs and such, dealing with private emotions. A folksong repertoire comprises an assembly of tunes and texts performed in certain styles and in conditions of change it seems that it's the styles that are the most fragile, the most open to transformation. When you talk to people obsessed with notions of authenticity you find, more often than not, it's really style that they're talking about.

In countries where folksong traditions survive best among rural communities, industrialization means a crisis in what outsiders consider as the authentic. Old ways of performance become unsatisfactory to communities whose lives are taking on new shapes and new tempos. It's a venerable process, in fact. We forget that folk music has its own history as surely as art music has. Folksongs have been changing all the while. Otherwise in the Anglo-Saxon world we'd still be singing melodies based on a 3-note scale and banging a couple of sticks together as an accompaniment. Innovation is nothing new. We all know those folksong purists, and if they'd been on the go 2000 years or more ago, imagine their consternation when the bagpipe first appeared on the scene—two voices from one instrument; they'd have said "Unauthentic! A violation of tradition!"

So traditions have been changing all the time. The only difference between then and now is that nowadays the changes are more drastic and they happen faster. It's a process that involves pluses and minuses, like most changes. As folksong becomes more and more a matter of public performance, it tends to gain in surface brilliance and to lose in true emotional depth. It's a dilemma that's worried the minds of many people caught up in the folksong revival, described by Kenny Goldstein a short time ago, when a sizeable proportion, especially of young people, feel that the panic and emptiness of so much pop music is, in the long run, poor fare, and they look to the values of the old folksong tradition for a bit more nourishment. But in present-day circumstances, when music is made specifically for listening to instead of as a means of getting things done, the question of style, of presentation, comes to the forefront. Some revivalists, not wanting to upset things too much, opt for a style that closely resembles, even imitates the style of past societies. At the other end of the spectrum, some bold spirits feel that modern electronic treatments allow songs to speak more clearly to present-day audiences: firstly, because electric music is the popular prestige music of the day, to which the musical ear of millions is tuned; and secondly, because amplification means that it is within the power of a mere quartet or quintet of good musicians to convey a degree of elation or terror that's far beyond the power of most symphony orchestras, and to do so without taking the music away from the social class that created and carried that music in the past. It's a hazardous venture, of course. But in Britain it was our good fortune that several musicians who were tempted into the electric field were people who, through their experiences in the more modest regions of the folksong revival, had acquired a genuine respect for the melody and poetry of traditional folksong.

The tendency to transport folksong lock, stock, and barrel into the world of electronics really began during the latter part of the 1960s, and the first big "all-electric, all-folksong" concert was presented in London in 1969 by the Fairport Convention Band, led by a gnomelike and somewhat gnomic fiddler, Dave Swarbrick, with a sweet, plump lady to whom I was devoted, Sandy Denny, as vocalist. Swarbrick said he was attracted to amplified music because he liked the sound, and because it offered great possibilities of exploring the dramatic content of the songs. With what success? You may judge from this first example, a somewhat enigmatic song called "Reynardine." Music Example: "Reynardine" (Island, ILPS 9115).

The electric band that captured the most public attention, sold the most records, and appeared most frequently on television was one called Steeleye Span. It was formed in 1970 and for a long time resisted the temptation of the rock world. In some respects it remained closer to tradition than Fairport, until about 1974 or so when a drummer was imported. As a couple of their instrumentalists wanted to revert to acoustic music, the band replaced them with a couple of rock musicians and the music became heavier and the presentation became more showy, involving dances, especially from the vocalist Maddy Prior in her daintily-held long dress. They went into back-projection film, and incorporated a mummers' play in their show. They were a decent band in their day.

The folk revival, from the first, had favored a repertoire drawn from the more subversive aspects of the traditional fund of songs. For instance, one of Fairport's great successes was a song about a deserter from the army. Steeleye found, a bit to their surprise, that a song from the early eighteenth century satirizing royalty was considered a big crowd-pleaser. Steeleye Span had always been strong with dance-like tunes, and the catchy rhythm and the melodic surprises of a song called "Cam Ye o'er frae France?" ("Did you come over from France?") were doubtless what struck the audience. It can hardly have been the words, certainly, which still remain cryptic even if one understands the dialect. Still it was clear that it mocks the King of England, newly arrived from Germany, and his plump mistress. Music Example: "Cam Ye o'er frae France?" (Chrysalis CHR 1046 B).

So it happened that songs opposed to war were, and still are, common in the repertoire of our electric folk bands. A feature of many of these bands is that at a certain stage in the performance the singer ceases and the band takes over in a fairly extended interlude, as it were, to reinforce the mood of the song or even to change its atmosphere. Professor Goldstein referred to singer Walter Pardon, who comes from near Walsham, Norfolk. Many years ago Vaughan Williams was notating folksongs in the Walsham area. He found it musically very rich, and he notated a beautiful song there, called "Lovely on the Water." It concerns a sailor saying good-bye to his girl. It goes along very pleasantly, very springlike—nothing passionate. The sailor has to sail away on a warship because the country is at war. It's quite sweet and lyrical until the last verse, which has a striking image: the celebrated Tower of London is on a hill, Tower Hill, and Tower Hill has been for centuries very much associated with seamen (when I was working as a seaman I used to get paid off on Tower Hill), and the last verse says that Tower Hill is crowded with women weeping sore for their sweethearts who've gone to face "the cannons' thunderous roar," or words to that effect. So the mood of the song has changed, but before the mood changes the band threateningly prepares one for this transformation in an interesting but, nowadays for our electric bands, very characteristic fashion. Music Example: "Lovely on the Water" (B&C Records CAS 1029).

As such bands will, Fairport and Steeleye Span and the other big electric bands of ten years or so ago have folded, refolded, folded again, disappeared temporarily, looked like disappearing permanently and then reemerging. At present, neither Fairport nor Steeleye Span is in existence. but may be again at any moment. In the meantime new bands are appearing, especially in Scotland, and some are of considerable interest. They're often a little too heavy for what they have to say, just at present. These things are always a delicate matter.

I'd like to end this dissertation with a band that has relatively newly appeared on the scene, called Five Hand Reel. At present it is a mixture of players from the north of Ireland and from Scotland. They're singing a song that has American associations and indeed is known in America—"Paddy's Green Shamrock Shore." I think perhaps they make a bit more of it than the song really carries, but at the same time it's an interesting enough exercise. Music Example: "Paddy's Green Shamrock Shore" (Topic 12TS 406).

So there, with varying success, you may feel, is a little panorama of at least one aspect (one only) of our extremely variegated folksong revival.

PART II
Ethnic Voices

How the Fiddler Got on the Roof

Mark Slobin

ACROSS THE WORLD the emergence of a commercial popular music based on folk sources is a sure sign of modernization. In Western Europe the impulse began as early as Elizabethan England, spreading out in wave-like fashion first to Eastern Europe, then to the vast global reaches of the colonial powers. The Russian Empire felt the stirrings of this movement relatively late, well into the nineteenth century. For the Jews of Eastern Europe, a repressed subculture within that imperial world, it was not until the 1870s that an autonomous ethnic popular musical style developed.[2] It was closely tied to the emergence of the Yiddish theater, the group's major modern form of entertainment. The birth and flourishing of secular literature in Yiddish, the colloquial language, is also coincidental with these trends. Developments in theater, literature, and music all drew on a similar intellectual base: the "Jewish Enlightenment" (*Haskala*). This secularizing cultural movement began in Germany and spread eastward, striving to bring the isolated Jewish population into the mainstream of European culture.

Not accidentally, all of this activity occurred at the same historical moment which witnessed a relentless pull of the Jews towards urbanization and proletarianization. The *shtetl*, or small town, so vividly (and inaccurately) portrayed in *Fid-*

dler on the Roof, lost its preeminence as locus of Jewish culture, with the center of gravity shifting towards the metropolis, with Warsaw, Kiev, and Odessa setting the pace. The Jews began to participate in mass social movements: socialism and Zionism. Meanwhile, persecution intensified. The assassination of Czar Alexander III in 1881 unleashed a series of devastating pogroms which propelled two million Jews to leave for America. Thus, emigration and the growth of popular culture evolved inextricably. Eventually New York became the nerve center of musical and theatrical activity, making Jewish popular music a markedly American phenomenon.

From the very outset this new layer of Jewish music culture was eclectic and multichanneled, tied to the immediate issues, languages, and musical idioms of the day. Popular music combined traditions that might seem mutually exclusive: the Yiddish folksong, the music of the synagogue, the popular music of the surrounding non-Jewish world, and European classical music, especially opera. Not surprisingly, given the complex history of the Eastern European Jews, each one of these styles is, in turn, an eclectic one. The Yiddish folksong, for example, is a blend of Western and Eastern European musical resources and Jewish sensibilities. The Jews' interest and ability in choosing from a wide offering of available musics—which is what eclecticism really means—led to a rich layering of styles from which a handful of talented songwriters fashioned a new ethnic tradition. Chief among these men was Abraham Goldfadn (1840-1908), who is officially credited with founding the Yiddish theater in Rumania in 1876.

Goldfadn himself described how he concocted the "scores" (largely unwritten or, at least, unorchestrated) for his early works.[3] He refused to call these musical dramas "operas," since the music was not the product of a single composer. He would sit in Rumanian cafes and, though musically illiterate, absorb the tunes of various Balkan ethnic groups. Later, in Odessa (ca. 1880), he would frequent the nightclubs of Armenians and Greeks for "exotic" material to represent the Jews'

Near Eastern Biblical past. At the same time, he would summon local *meshoyrerim* (choirboys, or cantorial assistants) to bring books of sacred music for use as source material. Among opera composers he singles out Verdi, Meyerbeer, and even Wagner as musical goldmines for his works. Simultaneously he fell back on Jewish and non-Jewish folksong to create musical dramas that became the great warhorses of the Yiddish stage, consisting of a finely-balanced mixture of comedy, melodrama, and music. Some of Goldfadn's creations became folksongs in their own right for later generations of both European and American Jews.

Goldfadn also collaborated with Sigmund Mogulesco (1855-1914), often called the "Jewish Charlie Chaplin" for his comic genius but also recognized as a major songwriter in the early Yiddish theater. A Mogulesco aria of 1897 (Example 1) can give us a sense of the style of this fledgling period of Jewish-American popular music. It comes from the show *David's Violin (Dovids fidele)*, one of the most popular works of Joseph Lateiner, a theatrical wizard who crafted some two hundred dramas with music. This is the key song, "Dor holekh ve dor bo," from Act IV. David, a musician, convinces Tevya, his brother, not to hang himself—Tevya is healed through "the magic power of music," the play's subtitle. A sound recording issued on Columbia in 1917[4] indicates the durability of popular music: the song was apparently commercially viable a full generation after the show's premiere. Such persistence demonstrates how popular music itself becomes a tradition, its styles and metaphors seeping imperceptibly into the culture.

The opening of "Dor holekh" has a strong cantorial flavor, sung on the record in a quite free rhythm with a recitative delivery. The following section blends folk and operatic sounds, delivered with a sobbing liturgical voice. Taken as a whole, the song has a cultural resonance best described by the Yiddish adjective *heymish*, comparable to what blues singers might call a downhome sound (Example 1).

By the time "Dor holekh" was recorded, the early style of

Jewish-American popular music had changed drastically. Plays about domestic tragedy and Old World persecution slowly yielded to more contemporary plots about life in the United States. Just as the Jewish community began to search for linguistic and social solutions in the New World, so its composers became absorbed by updating the musical idiom. In the context of a brief survey we can touch on only two principal trends of modernization. First, songwriters aimed at a genteel, classical style epitomized by the continental operetta, as represented in America by Victor Herbert. Second, obvious references to the colloquial American musical vocabulary make their presence known. We will cite sample songs to illustrate both facets of the new sound.

Example 1. "Dor holekhve dor bo" from *David's Violin* (1897, Mogulesco)

Our first example is from the work of Joseph Rumshinsky (1881-1944), a major trend-setter in the teens and early twenties. His name is closely linked to the attempt to "uplift" the Yiddish musical stage. At the time when Rumshinsky first began to work in New York (1906), men like Mogulesco still dominated the theater. These striking activists were musically semiamateur, having received their tutelage in the old cantorial apprenticeship system, and could function simultaneously as actors, musicians, singers, directors, or even stagehands. Rumshinsky, on the other hand, had worked hard at mastering the technique of classical European music, and was later cited as being the first real professional in the American Yiddish theater.[5] Eventually he was to gain the nickname "the Jewish Victor Herbert." In 1911, Rumshinsky wrote the score for *Shir hashirim* ("Song of Songs"), which has been called the first Yiddish operetta based solely on the topic of romantic love, in contrast to the preceding historical and domestic melodramas. In the song titled "Gavotte," he self-consciously displayed mainstream compositional craft. The song was recorded by Regina Zuckerberg,[6] one of the figurative and literal heavyweights of the Yiddish stage, who carefully enunciated the text and delivered the high-tessitura melody flawlessly (Example 2).

Example 2. "Gavotte" from *Shir hashirim* (1911, Rumshinsky)

The second major trend cited above, Americanization, has many sides. Often songs on blatantly American topics, like the women's suffrage movement, were automatically coded in an up-to-date idiom. An examination of the huge trove of manuscript musical items housed at the YIVO Institute for Jewish Research[7] shows just how pervasive this tendency could be. One turns up occasional stage directions scribbled in by conductors, such as "Yanke Dudil in G." The third example illustrates this trend. It is an excerpt from a World War I song, "Onkl sem" ("Uncle Sam"). The First World War posed a serious challenge to American Jewry, who were called upon to fight for their new homeland, possibly against their own relatives in Germany and Austria-Hungary. Mainstream American songs, such as immigrant songwriter Irving Berlin's "Let's All Be Americans Now," urged ethnic Americans to shoulder arms for the United States while putting aside Old World loyalties. Jewish composers working within the community joined the move towards patriotism. The war gave Lower East Side composers license to toss in American references, including material from both standard items, such as "The Star-Spangled Banner," and newer pieces like the flag-waving tunes of George M. Cohan. "Onkl sem" does both. Beginning in the older, minor-key vein of the earlier Yiddish popular song, the tune suddenly shifts to a quotation from the national anthem, followed by the closing bars of Cohan's "You're a Grand Old Flag" (Example 3).[8]

In the 1920s, Jewish-American songwriters worked in a new cultural atmosphere. With the end of the era of mass immigration (1924), they could no longer count on a steady stream of fresh Yiddish-speaking theatergoers. In addition, the process of assimilation had accelerated: Jews no longer lived only in the old core neighborhood of New York (Lower East Side), and began to abandon the pattern of life which had fostered the older styles of entertainment. To attract an audience, composers and actors would have to make sure that their product matched the public's changing taste.

Example 3. "Onkl Sem" (1917)

It was at this point that Molly Picon, still an active performer today in her eighties, appeared on the scene. Vivacious and petite, she contrasted sharply with the Zuckerberg generation of ponderous prima donnas, and her music was as carefully tailored as her stereotyped costumes. Picon's memorable roles often fell into two categories. Small and slight, she could don the outfit of the *yeshiva-bokher*, the perennial male religious student of Eastern Europe, who now figured as a character in light comedy rather than turgid melodrama. Her finest film role, *Yidl mitn fidl*, also played on this cute sexual ambiguity. She also emerged as the lively romantic lead in musicals crafted especially for her by her husband, Yakov Kalich. In her routines, down to concerts given today, she draws on the Goldfadn era as point zero on the Jewish popular music scale straight through the sounds of jazz, exhibiting a versatility of which Goldfadn would have been proud. Despite the novelty of this approach, the early Picon sound relied on continuity in ethnic language and imagery, which increasingly included nostalgia for the European world of the past. In a number like "Mayn zeydes nign" ("Grandpa's Tune"), she could take an Old World melody of the deeply-felt, contemplative genre called *nign* and present it in three forms: first, the way Grandpa used to sing it (nostalgia), second as Grandpa's kids in the new Soviet Russia sing it (a la Russe), and finally as it sounds in New York (Broadway).

In another vein, Picon could also appeal to the younger set by imitating the French cabaret style then popular in America. In "Vox zol ikh tun az ikh hob im lib" ("What Can I Do? I Love Him") she takes as her model Fannie Brice's Ziegfield Follies rendition of Mistinguett's Parisian classic chanson, "Mon homme" ("My Man"). To hear Picon adapt Brice, of course, is to witness a great artist of the internal ethnic world paying tribute to a singer who chose the path of external success. Brice herself provided a model of the export brand of eclecticism, switching roles easily from the Jewish caricature of "Second Hand Rose of Second Avenue" to the Continental charm of "My Man," ending her career imitating a child on radio as Baby Snooks. Though the subject is far from our present topic, the success of Brice, Jolson, Cantor & Co. ought to be considered in the light of the eclectic in-group entertainment tradition that is the focus of the present paper.

In the 1930s Jewish-American popular music reached its full flowering in the work of such songwriting geniuses as Sholom Secunda, Abraham Ellstein, and Alexander Olshanetsky. Some of their hits even crossed over to the mainstream American scene. "Bay mir bist du sheyn" can still be heard in airports and elevators, the ultimate tribute American musical culture can pay in terms of durable success. A glance at the opening bars of a typical Ellstein hit, "Ikh zing" ("I Sing," 1937) (Example 4), written for the flourishing Yiddish movie wave, can typify the style. Completely nonethnic in musical content, the song relies on the cultural references encoded in its text for in-group identification. "Ikh zing far dir mayn shir hashirim" ("I Sing my Song of Songs for you") carries on the equation of Biblical-ethnic that we saw drawn upon for the title of Rumshinsky's 1911 musical on romantic love.[9]

Example 4. "Ikh zing" from *Mamale* (1937, Ellstein)

How the Fiddler Got on the Roof

After World War II, paired historical events of enormous consequence shaped the ethnic consciousness of American Jewry. The Holocaust annihilated the Old World, severing the always productive tie to Europe and sealing the fate of Yiddish-language entertainment. The creation of the State of Israel in 1948 brought in a new style and new cultural themes based on the triumph of the Zionist movement. Even the aging Al Jolson put out a hastily-concocted song called "Israel." Eventually, visiting troupes from Israel (which still pop up regularly) could stage Yiddish-language shows in New York, ironically importing the "Old World" from the newest zone of Jewish cultural energy.

Yet the basic trend was towards ever greater Americanization. In the 1950s the Latin dance craze swept America, but proved particularly long-lasting in the Jewish community. Even today, club-date musicians say they must tack on Latin numbers for Jewish weddings in greater New York, but not for other ethnic groups.[10] At the same time, the Barry Sisters (modeled on the Andrews Sisters) continued to translate American songs into Yiddish. In the 1970s they produced a long-playing record consisting completely of such crossovers, singing standards like "Tea for Two" and "Raindrops Keep Falling on my Head" in the Old World tongue, which shows just how thin the ethnic thread can be stretched.

By 1964, one might have predicted the appearance of an English-language musical designed for a Broadway audience, combining ethnic continuity, now completely couched in terms of nostalgia, with skillful use of an almost completely American idiom, in terms of both musical and cultural content. And so the fiddler was raised to the roof. Solid Broadway craftsmanship and ethnic charm combined to make the show a hit in places like Japan. The music of *Fiddler on the Roof* is not terribly ethnic, and there are gross distortions of the Sholom Aleichem stories that form the plot base.[11] Nevertheless, the underlying process is tried and true. Goldfadn might have been proud of Bock and Harnick, the songwriters.

The old dream that the founder of the Yiddish stage cherished of lending respectability to Jewish ethnic drama was modest indeed when compared to the international acclaim for *Fiddler*.

Having reached this phase, where could Jewish-American popular music go? There have been no challengers or successors to that landmark musical. In 1980 the pop singer Neil Diamond released his remake of the 1927 Jolson classic, *The Jazz Singer*, and went so far as to make the canonical bow to tradition by singing that holiest of Jewish chants, *Kol Nidre*, as Jolson did before him. Yet the plot has Diamond reject his pious, if mousey, Jewish wife and end up happily wedded to a non-Jewish woman as Sir Laurence Olivier, in the role of the singer's cantor-father, beams. In the rest of the soundtrack, Diamond carefully avoids any attempt at regenerating an ethnic style. In the process he introduced a couple of bland hit songs: success clearly is not meant to lie in in-group revitalization. It will take a Neil Diamond, or perhaps a once-again-Jewish-born Bob Dylan, to put new life into Jewish-American popular music. For the moment, "Hava Nagila," another airport favorite, briefly introduced in *The Jazz Singer* of 1980, stands firm as the basic trademark of ethnicity.

Yet one silver lining gleams in the "neo-*klezmer* movement." Young Jewish-American musicians (and some "converts") who come out of the American/Balkan folk revival movement have begun to play the instrumental dance tunes of the *klezmer*, the professional Jewish musician of Eastern Europe. These new folk reformulate the old wedding tunes and raucous Rumanian hoedown music of the Old World past as filtered through the scratchy 78s of 1920s immigrant musicians. To a certain extent there has been a standoff between these young revivalists and their hoped-for public. Many wedding guests sit back and wait for an Ellstein hit, "Hava Nagila," or a tune from *Fiddler*. Yet the movement grows,

How the Fiddler Got on the Roof

and perhaps someday the fiddler will jump down from the roof, stand once again in the village square, and play for the new ethnic celebration.

[1] The original version of this paper, read at the "Folk Music and Modern Sound" conference, was enlivened by a series of taped examples which could not be reproduced here. Unfortunately, there is no easy discography for much of the music under discussion.

[2] For a full account of early Jewish popular music, see my *Tenement Songs: The Popular Music of the Jewish Immigrants* (University of Illinois Press, 1982).

[3] See the entry under Goldfadn in Z. Zilbertsvayg, *Leksikon fun yidishn teater* (New York: Alisheva, 1931) for the cited material and a comprehensive biographical survey.

[4] Recorded by Morris Misheloff on Columbia E3105. Transcribed excerpt from the sheet music edition of 1897 (New York: Hebrew Publishing Co.). For convenience, all subsequent examples have been transcribed with *g* as tonic.

[5] These views of Rumshinsky emerge in the jubilee volume published for his fiftieth birthday *Dos rumshinsky-bukh* (New York: No publisher, 1931).

[6] Recorded on Victor 67920; transcription excerpt by ear from the disc.

[7] See my forthcoming article on this massive and fascinating archive in *YIVO Annual of Jewish Social Science*, 18 (New York: YIVO Institute for Jewish Research, 1982).

[8] Recorded by Louis Birnbaum on Columbia E4033; transcription excerpt by ear.

[9] Excerpt from *Jan Peerce on 2nd Avenue* (Vanguard VSD-79166), transcription by ear. The song was written by Ellstein with lyrics by Picon for her 1937 film vehicle *Mamale*, a joint Polish-American production.

[10] See Bruce MacLeod's "Music for All Occasions: The Club Date Business of Metropolitan New York" (PhD. dissertation, Wesleyan University, 1979).

[11] An analysis of *Fiddler* vs. Sholom Aleichem appears in my "Intersections of Jews, Music, and Theater" in a forthcoming anthology on Jews on stage and screen edited by Sarah B. Cohen (University of Illinois, in press).

Slovenian Style in Milwaukee

Charles Keil

WHEN OUR FRIEND, downstairs neighbor, colleague, and polka book collaborator, Dick Blau, left our American Studies in Buffalo to create and administer some fine arts in Milwaukee, we looked forward to expanding our polka horizons. Sure enough, after a time, we were invited to a conference on ethnic studies and the arts that would pay our way to Wisconsin and give us a few days to investigate some very disturbing clues to missing persons and mistaken identities. For, according to Dick and the people who were giving him his ethnic orientation to Milwaukee, Polish-American polka bands were conspicuous by their absence and, on the other hand, a considerable number of musicians with Polish last names were to be found playing in the bands and musical organizations of other ethnic groups. All this would not have seemed so mysterious if the Poles were just one small minority group among many trying to find their way in "a German town," but, in fact, the Poles were easily the largest ethnic group in the city with a population approaching half a million. A large Polish population in the city and in the city's surrounding suburbs and in the farm country west and north was surely one of the reasons why the International Polka Association had chosen Milwaukee for its convention and festival five years in a row. But the continuing presence of the IPA convention only deepened the mystery. How could Milwaukee be a polka center, host to the big event of the year, and not have any bands of its own? Polish bands, that is.

For it soon became apparent, after the conference, that there were plenty of polka bands in Milwaukee, all of them Slovenian, so the question to follow in a few days of fieldwork was two sided: why no Polish bands and why so many Slovenian?

The broad outlines of an explanation seemed to be fairly obvious. Milwaukee was famous for being a German city, a city that could make various brands of beer famous; the Germans were famous for pushing around Slavs and trying to fit them to their mold; the Slovenes were famous for being the most German oriented of the Slavic speaking peoples. So the Poles, outnumbered and "outclassed" by the earlier German immigrants and their Slovenian allies had lost out, either in skirmishes and battles of the *Kultur Kampf* that extended to a Milwaukee front, or through slow steady American acculturation pressures intensified by very successful German and Slovenian neighbors. Unfortunately, conversations with conference participants from Milwaukee didn't offer much specific substantiation for this theory. The Poles were reported to be quite solid in their South Side parishes, well represented politically, doing all right economically, just not so visible culturally or musically. The Germans were not any more visible than the Poles, having had their high morale of the nineteenth century lowered severely by World War I and eliminated by World War II. The Slovenes were never a large population, were split by factions of some kind, and had lost their old neighborhood to the Mexicans and Puerto Ricans twenty years ago. Yet their style was the people's music of Milwaukee. Why?

The day after the conference I wandered down Lincoln Avenue, in the heart of the Polish neighborhoods, not really knowing what I was looking for. As always, the churches were impressive. I passed a basilica that was certainly a fit place for the Pope to hang his hat if he should come to Milwaukee. And every corner had its tavern. Polonia. I stopped awhile at a big old music store that had probably seen better

days. The record racks had old albums I'd never seen before—
"Gene Wisniewski Presents Walt Jaworski and Eddie Olinski,"
coming from an era when a Connecticut bandleader's introduction could help two Buffalo bands find work out of town;
an old Solek album with terrific pictures of Walt in twenty
different costumes on the cover; records by other Buffalo
bands—Big Steve, the New Yorkers playing Rhinelanders—on
Lil' Wally's Jay Jay label, that I never knew existed. There
were many rows of 45s as well, with titles and leaders' names
neatly tabbed. I began to look around for the 78s and a listening booth to try them in. As it turned out, there were still
a few booths in the back of the store used for storage, but
the big inventory of 78s had been divided between a collector
and the junkman a few years earlier. An old employee who
played many years with Max and the Merrymakers and who
could have answered my questions about the Polish bands
had passed on last year. Though many hundreds of Polonia's
young musicians had taken lessons there, it was too late for
me to learn a lot.

I continued along Lincoln Avenue. More bars, some with
rock bands, others advertising C & W...the office of Representative Clement J. Zablocki...the Polish Roman Catholic
Union of America office up over a tavern...funeral home...
Roman's Jewelers. Does every Polonia have a Roman who is a
jeweler? Then I came to Jimmy Maupin's tavern with pictures
of people playing accordions in the window. Time for a beer
and brandy.

The bar was deserted when I went in, no regulars, apparently the kind of place that exists mostly for the weekend
nights, but it wasn't quitting time yet. A man came up front
and served me a beer as I explained my search for Polish bands
in Milwaukee. Jimmy introduced himself with the brandy and
presented his credentials as Frankie Yankovic's second accordion player for many years and leader of his own Slovenian
style band. I pushed the button on my tape recorder.

CK: *Why so many Slovenian bands in Milwaukee?*
JM: Honestly, it was all Frankie. He hit big with "Blue Skirt

Slovenian Style in Milwaukee

Waltz" and "Just Because" back in '47 or '48 and it's been that way ever since. Before Frankie, say 50 years ago, the north side of Milwaukee was all accordion music, button boxes, German music, and south of the viaduct it was Polish concertinas. There wasn't any big Slovenian community in Milwaukee. I'll be honest with you. I lived in Milwaukee all my life and I didn't know what a Slovenian was. To me that was probably Czechoslovakia; I never heard of Yugoslavia, but Frankie changed all that.

CK: *You discovered there were Slovenians in Milwaukee?*

JM: Yeah, they brought him in. There was a tightknit old community, say from 1st to 16th Streets and from Pierce Street to roughly Greenfield, where it's all Spanish now. They held all their doings out at Arcadian Park or a place called Turner Hall. And Frankie packed 'em in, not all Slovenians, of course, they hosted him. He was like their hero and everybody else came around.

CK: *But what was there before Frankie in '47? Just concertinas and accordions, no bands?*

JM: That was about it. Of course, I'm 45 now, I was about drinking age when Frank first came to town with "Blue Skirt." But I think the Poles just had their concertinas, with maybe sax and drums, no big bands, just Milwaukee-style Polish music. I remember Max and the Merrymakers because they were on every Tuesday night from the Wisconsin Roof Ballroom for years and years, about 30 years, ten or eleven pieces, more of a dance band that played a lot of everything. And Irv Mattey had a well-known band, I think it was maybe two concertinas, a horn and drums. A couple of other bands. Hey, you should get ahold of Fritz the Plumber for examples, all the early bands, he has 'em, Norman Margoff at WYLO. He could sort things out for you.

At this point, an old timer came in with an old accordion and overhearing our conversation, he stated flatly and swiftly:

> I was the first commercial polka bandleader in this area! There was polkas for a coupla thousand years, but that was only weddings and parties. I organized it. I had Maupin here playing for me in '48 and '49, didn't I, Jimmy? (Maupin nods a sincere 'yes' but gives me a smile that says it's not quite like he's telling it.) And George Baltz on accordion, a German, but he played by ear, everything. We had bass fiddle, drums, banjo, but there wasn't a well-known Polish polka band in Milwaukee. There was the Jolly Polecats, you'd have to say they were number one for awhile, but they played Slovenian music and they were Italian! All five Italians, all five of 'em, every damn one of 'em.

Jimmy started to tell me about Chet Ubick and the Ubick Brothers, a strictly Polish band that was popular after the war, but the old timer would have none of it.

> Frankie hit it with "Blue Skirt" and them Italians smelled a buck. If you want straight Polish, you gotta go to Pulaski, Wisconsin. They play it all day long in the taverns, all night, too. Like they do rock down here. Polkas, polkas, polkas. One hundred fifty miles from here, 154 miles to be exact, Green Bay to Route 32. Bandleaders run the place. Dick Rodgers owns half the town, he's a Polak, don't let the "Rodgers" fool ya, and Alvin Stasinski owns half the farms. Put them two together in a knot. Nothing like that here in Milwaukee. It's all Slovenian here. The originals before Yankovic even were Slovenians. I'd say Frankie Bevsek was on top for a while, and Rudy Pugel, and Louie Bashell, he's on top now. Pugel's dead and Bevsek is retired.

CK: *Those are all Slovenian names? What about Maupin? What's your background?*

JM: Well, basically, Irish and German and some Indian. It's good to have that Indian, you know, they can't deport you. My father was Kelly, a railroad man, and my mother was from West Bend, but I was adopted.

Slovenian Style in Milwaukee 37

The old timer jumped in again:

> You know, he's more adopted by the Slovenians than anybody else; because they actually think he is a Slovenian. You know that yourself, Jimmy.

Sensing, perhaps, that the old timer was running away with the interview again, Maupin asked him about the accordion case he was carrying and, indeed, that was the basic purpose of his afternoon visit, to get the recently repaired accordion checked out by Jimmy before turning it over to his son. This led to a technical discussion of accordions. In the case was an original "musette" style accordion built by George Karpek's father. George, who had just repaired it, built the special "no-bass" accordion for Lawrence Welk (wunnerful, I wonder if his left hand never learned to play because it always wanted to conduct). The owner of this antique explained that all real polka accordions are "musette" or "wet-tuned," because "it gives more polka bounce to the music, see, originally they had buttons." Before I could get too confused, Jimmy played a few bright polka choruses and explained:

JM: See, it sounds louder up to 25 feet away, because it's really slightly out of tune, it's shrill, the waves go out like this (gestures of overlapping waves) but after 25 feet, it defeats itself because you're not playing a true tone. The wet-tuned sounds sharp to the ear. I like a dry tuning because I have an amplifier, perfect pitch at 76 degrees in 80 percent humidity. I always liked that sound and it was Frank's sound. He was amplified from 1952 or so on, and before that it was stand mikes, so you could say he was amplified from the start.

As the old timer packed up the accordion and headed for the door, he said, "Tell him about the first time you ran your hand down the accordion and Frankie said, 'Don't you ever do *that* again.' "

JM: It's true, you know. One of the first times I played with Frank in 1958, I got excited and did a run, a gliss really, down the keyboard, and Frank turned around and said that, and meant it. He wanted to hear every note in every run.

CK: *You were playing a lot of runs with Frankie? Tell me about his style. How would you describe it?*

JM: Sure. Single note runs are the only thing that works. We tried doing little things with harmonies but it doesn't sound right. So the second accordion plays the fills; he plays twice as many notes each night as the lead. Lead sticks to the melody, with some harmony maybe, and the second can play harmony, or harmony over the melody, or maybe a counter melody, and all those single note runs that fill up the spaces. I ride off of what Frank is doing.

CK: *Mainly those runs. What do you do with your left hand?*

JM: Not much really. It's basically just the two right hands, two balanced accordions. Real simple. Really, I like all kinds of music but Slovenian comes easiest. Basic peasant simplicity is best. But clean. Clean and sharp. You want to hear every note.

CK: *So with Frank you had two accordions plus bass and banjo?*

JM: Right. Simplicity. You can listen to the melody. It's easy to dance to. You know, with the banjo in 4, Slovenian music seems to flow, Frankie's style, Cleveland style, whatever you want to call it, it flows.

CK: *What about drums? Don't you have to have drums?*

JM: I have drums in my group now and no banjo, but almost all the Slovenian bands have banjo, usually he doubles guitar for other stuff, like country songs. But Frank didn't take drums on the road, took up too much room in the car and took too long to set up once you got there. You have to understand, all Frank's work was touring, one month, five months, two months. I hit all 49 states with Frankie over about a ten-year period, and the four of us with instruments, suitcases, amps, could just fit in the station wagon. Always on the road. If Frank plays in Cleveland, forget it. Slovenians are funny people, awful jealous of each other. I'll tell you that 90 percent of the people Frank plays to are Polish, just like most of the people who come in here are Polish.

CK: *Who else comes in?*

JM: Some German, some Slovenian, about 75 percent Polish, it's a Polish neighborhood; a few Croatians, a few Mexicans.

CK: *Mexicans?*

JM: We got some Mexicans down here, too; they filled in where the Slovenians were and the Slovenes went out to West Allis, West Milwaukee. Now there's a guy—Doc Perko's place is on the border between two, he grew up on National Avenue and knows the thirties and forties. He can talk for hours about the music then.

CK: *I'll try to look him up. Is there much friction between all the different groups?*

JM: Yes. Between the Mexicans and Puerto Ricans. They look down on each other.

CK: *I was thinking more of the people who come in here.*

JM: Not really. Everybody gets along, has a good time. It's just that you'll never change a Polish mind. They won't cross the line. Most Polish equate a Mexican with a knife and a mustache. The Polish can't understand how the Mexican is more fatalistic, blows all his money on a Saturday night 'cause maybe he won't be here on Monday. Whereas the Polish work hard to get where they are, he takes care of his lawn, he's clean, keeps to himself. It's their own Mexicans exploit the Mexicans most, believe me. A lot of wetbacks taking jobs from the Polish people doesn't help relations any. And then they don't pay taxes either, that really hurts. The Polish are very conscious of the taxes. Welfare checks are killing them.

CK: *So any frictions between the Slavic and Spanish communities are sort of built-in, coming from the economic side?*

JM: Yeah, I don't have any trouble in here. You know who could tell you a lot about Slovenes and Mexicans is Tony Beyer. Beyer isn't Polish, but he came out through Poland, I think, after the war and had the National Ballroom at 6th and National when the neighborhood was still Slovenian, but changing over. He's been sick a lot lately but his wife Zena would know. They booked strictly Mexican for a while, Latin, Mexican polka bands right where the Slovenian polka bands were. Ask the Beyers, ask for them out at the Blue Canary by the airport. They'll know.

CK: *I've never heard Mexican polkas, just about them. What's it like?*

JM: Beto Salinas is the best known around here, it's button accordion, wet-tuned, real staccato, like "Peanut Polka"—do you know that tune?

CK: *No, maybe I've heard it and didn't know it. So nobody from this community goes to Mexican polka dances or likes that style much?*

JM: I don't think so. Some old people are still living in the old neighborhood but they wouldn't be going to dances much.

CK: *With every community so attached to its own music, how was Frankie Yankovic able to take over Milwaukee?*

JM: "Blue Skirt Waltz" was a *big* hit, something over 2,000,000 copies over the years, I'll bet. You know, somebody else in Cleveland recorded it before Frankie but he had the promotion, I guess. And "Just Because" was a million seller. That's big time. Not just another polka band.

CK: *But what did he push aside so to speak, that were the established styles here?*

JM: I guess Lawrence Duchow was the biggest draw in the

Slovenian Style in Milwaukee   41

CK: area before Frank, sort of sweet German-Bohemian style.
CK: *I heard a 78 of his that sounded like Guy Lombardo.*
JM: Right. And Romy Gosz was big in the whole area, another Bohemian.
CK: *Lil' Wally was telling me that his trumpet could make you cry.*
JM: Cousin Fuzzy was coming up in the forties, also German style.
CK: *Well, why didn't the Polish South Side generate a lot of bands? I still can't figure it out.*
JM: I'll tell you what it is on the South Side. It's probably their independent nature. Instead of five or six ten-piece bands, you might have 200 three-piece bands. They were playing all the time, weddings 'n that, that was the big thing. So nobody really got organized outside of Max.
CK: *And after '47-'48, if you do get organized it will be in the Slovenian style?*
JM: Sure. You had to. That was the thing that was going.

We spent more time looking over Jimmy's albums of photographs and clippings, most of them documenting his work with Yankovic over the years. We discussed the finer points of Slovenian style as it has evolved in Cleveland and Milwaukee: Frankie Yankovic's range of keys and "patented endings" of an extra bar or two; the high standard set by Joe Trolli's early arrangements for Frankie; the intense competition between excellent bands in Cleveland—Johnny Pecon's pride, the Vadnal's perfectionism, Timco's recent push to the top of the Cleveland pile. I formed the impression that everything important in Slovenian style polkas happened in Cleveland first. The pace, the actual tempo was faster there. Cleveland banjos were swinging in four while Milwaukee's still clumped along on the off beats. Perhaps the key factor in Yankovic's success in Milwaukee was the solidity of his Cleveland foundations. He took off because he had a better launching pad. The blend of competition and cooperation that it takes to make any music, any style, any culture cohere and then grow, was somehow better managed in Cleveland.

Leaving Maupin's and heading back to Blau's house for dinner, my head was full of Slovenian style as a set of interesting "problems in ethnomusicology." I couldn't, and still can't, hear it as the flowing, clean, and glowing thing that Maupin described. What was "flowing" and "clean" to him sounded stiff and a little sterile to me. But I knew from past experience that this was probably because I had not yet listened long enough to get inside the music. And, of course, my recently acquired bias for Am-Pol polkas was getting in the way. Yankovic's "Blue Skirt Waltz" swept Milwaukee in 1947; my interest in the why and how of that kept me from hearing what Jimmy was saying about the "independent nature" of the South Side Polish and their "200 three-piece bands." Listening to the tapes and writing about our Milwaukee trip a few years later, I am sure those two little phrases eliminate a lot of unnecessary mystery. Polish traditions were probably strong for a long time inside the community but weak outside it, strong because the old country village traditions of small "pick-up groups" for weddings and parties were maintained in the parishes, weak in that there was no demand (indeed, probably considerable scorn) for such music outside Polonia in the German and Slovenian neighborhoods. Polish-American polkas were probably alive and well in Milwaukee through the forties and fifties but just not very audible or visible to the rest of the city.

I returned to the Blau house and met there one David Paul Winkler, known to his friends as "D. P." America's ethnic cities should be full of Winklers—"cosmopolitan workers," "organic intellectuals," how should we identify those people who get high on the histories, languages, and world views of their fellow citizens? As a philosophy major and bartender, D. P. likes to know about those forces and events in Austro-Hungarian history that might account for some of the emo-

Slovenian Style in Milwaukee

tions bottled up inside his older patrons. As a lover of fine wines and musics, he has to find out where Milwaukee's "best vintages" and "village bands" are located. Why? Maybe because his people were from contested Poznan. Maybe because his grandfather insisted on English being spoken in the home but kept a large picture of the Kaiser over the piano throughout World War I. Such threads of explanation would fit with D. P.'s own predilection for getting to the nineteenth-century root of things. But why do so few want to remember while so many want to forget? A hard question for "new ethnicity" and old ethnicity theorists alike and one that D. P. couldn't answer either except to say that "America was made up of shit from the start; all the respectable people stayed in Europe. The German '48ers who started this city were decent, but everybody else was running, poor, desperate. So why look back?"

CK: *Why do you?*

DP: I can't get enough of the "old style," old village styles like Goral fiddling, the minor keys, something barbaric about it. That's why I go for Chicago-style polkas, they still have some of that mountain music sound. John Zurawaki's band of old timers in Chicago had some of that East European sound. All the Chicago bands, the Ampolaires, even modern Eddie B. has some of it.

But what's interesting to me is how people talk about jazz, how a theme is picked up and how they keep going and working at it, but, hell, these clowns in the villages were doing that for a hundred years already. They start some little weirdo line, somebody stand up and chant out one verse or just one line and then they'd grab that and just grind on it till they'd exhausted the possibilities. A wild thing. Develop it, work it up into this great big bang!

CK: *So why doesn't this sound survive at all in Milwaukee? How did Frankie Yankovic sweep the field and establish himself so easily?*

DP: I think Yankovic created the first new sound, a silly thing to say, but in a sense he did. It was a complete mixture, taking all the old styles and just making this thing. Because what Yankovic plays is definitely not of any one ethnic background. I've always kidded about it and called it pretzel bending music because it was noncommittal. It wasn't the sound of a village in Upper Bavaria, or one in Slovenia, or a Bohemian village, or a Slovak village. It was one of the first things to come *out* of these old folk traditions; he sort of made it respectable. They didn't like it when Uncle John would get half juiced up, grab his fiddle and start sawing; that, you know... So Yankovic made it respectable—he irons it out, smooths it, not raw anymore—and other people picked it up. Now they don't make mistakes. Somebody doesn't kick over a drink, or break a string, it's all the straight poop. I would never say I dislike Frankie Yankovic, but that music doesn't move my spirit *at all*. It seems too mechanical to me.

From "a wild thing" to respectable perfectionism, from grabbing and grinding up a "great big bang" to the smooth, mechanical "straight poop." Yankovic would certainly not like this descriptive evaluation of his music, but he is proud of having cut the polka free of ethnicity. Says Frankie, "You see, I was trying to give the polka a certain beat where it wouldn't be tied to no ethnic group in particular. I never liked wind instruments. I found I had enough lead in the accordion."[1]

But it is "those wind instruments" that can keep the polka wild and Dionysian, a wailing clarinet or alto sax, the two trumpets of Chicago style. While an accordion is technically a wind instrument, it is not blown. And while two accordions, like two of any instrument, always produce a sum of overtones and harmonics greater than the parts played, the primary goal of Yankovic's music is clearly control—dry tuned "perfect pitch at 76 degrees and 80 percent humidity," not too hot, not too wet and mushy, and none of those excited glissandos, Mr. Maupin, please.

My own hot jazz biases and D. P. Winkler's similar feeling for the village sound could easily lead us astray here. Time to reassert a few basic points: Yankovic's music is (1) basically ethnic, i.e. Slovenian, but also somewhat black; (2) working class, and (3) one of the most popular polka styles to have appeared in America.

Taking these points in reverse order, the size of Frank's big hits in the forties and fifties suggest a large audience "waiting" for that sound, second generation people anxious to have their parents' old country passions Americanized—smoothed up, ironed out, machine tooled, in a word, modernized. Uncle John became an embarrassment; his passion to get into the music and get everyone else into it with him produced a lot of false starts, broken strings, and spilt drinks, all aspects of involvement. The second generation doesn't want to fetch another drink, wait for a string to be replaced, or participate psychologically in a false start even if that participation will be rewarded with a bigger bang at the end of the grind. Trying hard in public, what blacks used to call "soul," doesn't communicate to everyone any more. Passion makes for "mistakes," perhaps passion itself is a mistake—anyway, we want a finished product, say the children of the uprooted. And in the postwar boom ethnic America could afford to pay for it, would be happy to pay for it, happy to have jobs, happy the war was over, happy to dance the polka without having to worry about nurturing the music process.

Frankie Yankovic, or more accurately, Slovenian Cleveland, was able to effect this transformation of collective practice into professional product, this transformation of first generation ethnic working class passions into second generation ethnic working class perfectionism. This "perfecting" process is paralleled by all the other strong proletarian styles of this century[2]—Afro-American blues, Greek rebetika, Yoruba juju,—

and from studying these one could predict the essential characteristics of the Slovenian-American process. Describing this process for any of these styles with a set of ideal characteristics or material factors at work reduces the real complexity of what may have happened more or less simultaneously to a set of specifics that raise more or less valid sequential questions.[3] For example, from the set of four factors discussed below, can we determine which came first, "amplification" or "streamlining," "commodification" or "control"?

In trying to define these features a variety of answers emerge. The "amplification" factor makes a big difference in any style. Certainly it helps the Slovenian-Americans keep their bands small and mobile. It let Frankie Yankovic dispense with the blown and the beaten, those Dionysian wind instruments and drums. It allows the switch from shrill penetrating wet-tuned accordions to dry-tuned perfect pitch models. And improving PA systems in the thirties and forties encouraged instrumentalists to become more vocal, vocalists to become more lyrical and conversational.

The "commodification" factor pivots on the change that occurs in the recording studio when a people's practice becomes a company's product. In some styles this exerts a strong "perfecting" pressure, e.g. the three-minute time limit of the 78 RPM cuts a lot of conversation out of the blues, eliminates most of the *taxemia* (presentation of the modal "road" by the bouzouki player) from Greek rebetika, and cuts out or compresses the gradual tempo shifts of Yoruba juju. But I suspect that perfectionism was an element of Slovenian style before the era of recordings and that, for example, beginning together and ending together very precisely was not a feature taught to Slovenian bands by recording session supervisors. Careful interviewing of the older Slovenian stylists might reveal some basic recording studio constraints on the style, but beyond the general pressure not to make mistakes I doubt if anything specific could be documented. On the other side of the commodification equation, however, the power of promotion and distribution to increase consumption of the songs by an enlarged audience was certainly a force keeping the lyrics prominent and in English and probably a factor in keeping the band small so that Yankovic could tour easily to meet his new audiences.

Just as these first two factors, "amplification" and "commodification," can be boiled down to one complex efficient cause, electric technology's impact on a people's music, so the next two factors, "streamlining" and "control," could be reduced to a simple final cause or goal—happiness, feeling real and good, strong and in control of some new power. Song and dance can do that for people, temporarily, and it seems to be the case across cultures under capitalism, that the further and faster people lose control of their daily lives and working conditions (moving from farm to factory, from craft work to assembly line), the more they want to hear and feel control in their music. Alienated from their bodies during the working week, they require reintegration, recreation at the weekend polka dances. Their work/play dialectic shapes the style. The deep push for "control" in the music styles of the proletariat comes from the powerlessness of the working class but the specific forms control will take have an ethnic dimension that might be called "streamlining." A class/ethnic dialectic shapes the style, too.

Asking B. B. King's and Bobby Bland's fans in the early sixties (and in those days *all* their supporters were Afro-Americans) what they liked in the music, the answer was always, "He's made it mellow," "It's smooth," or "They've streamlined the blues, made it modern." In other words, they kept the old music, but distilled it, simplified it, controlled it, perfected it. Old wine in a new bottle, whether the distilleries are Afro-American and located in postwar Memphis and Los Angeles, or Slovenian and located in postwar Cleveland and Milwaukee.

The new Slovenian-American style, not really created by Yankovic, but certainly polished, promoted, and disseminated by him (with some assistance from His Master's Voice), is controlled, clean, modern, streamlined in the extreme. Two dry-tuned and balanced accordions for melody and countermelody, lead and fills; no slurs and glissandos, every eighth note run articulated; no mess in the superstructure. And the bottom? There is a difference in the beat because it's black, 1920s black but Afro-American for sure. Basically, a banjo downstroked in 4/4 time gives the music its drive. The bass moves inside this beat in 2, with occasional measures, pairs of measures and whole choruses in 4/4. The bass notes are not German oom-pah, back and forth, root and fifth, but moving all over the chords and beyond in the 4/4 choruses where the affinities with early Ellington and Basie are most obvious. It is this combining of sounds—clear, clean accordions running and bouncing along over the bass and banjo rhythm team (a white/black dialectic)—that constitutes "streamlining" and "control" in Yankovic's music. Finally, the vocals keep this perfected style accessible. Yankovic singing by himself sounds like you or me or anyone else and much of the time he is joined by one or more other singers who create a participatory sing-along effect. It is this sound, a higher synthesis of three dialectical American dilemmas (work/play, class/ethnic, and black/white) that captured Milwaukee in the postwar period.

In dialectics, whether Marxist, Hegelian, or Ancient Greek, a "higher synthesis" is never permanent, always becomes a thesis that will be met by an antithesis. Now, polka lovers, if Yankovic's Cleveland Slovenian sound is the thesis of the 1945-1950 period, what is the antithesis emerging 1950 to 1960?

That's right; crazy Lil' Wally's honky style from Polish Chicago. And the higher synthesis emerging from this confrontation of polka kings? Right again: Marion Lush and Eddie Blazonczyk, the styles where Dionysian passion and Apollonian perfectionism meet.

But let's finish our trip to Milwaukee. Talking with D. P. Winkler and Dick late into the night we covered topics rang-

Slovenian Style in Milwaukee 49

ing from D. P.'s Big Church Theory—the bigger the church the more despised the people—through the problems of school integration, to the history of Milwaukee under socialism for most of the century. Bits of information about the various ethnic communities in the city, portions of the conference proceedings, and my general impressions of the city itself began to fit into place. Milwaukee was exceptionally clean and decent—wonderful parks, great library system, fine transportation—not at all like rowdy Chicago or depressed Buffalo. So it deserved a clean, decent, rational polka style, a compromise in taste and tempo between slow German and fast Polish. Within well-ordered Milwaukee the ethnic groups were perhaps more conservative than usual, more clannish, more concerned with internal factions than with public relations. As ever, the Serbs and Croats were at each other's throats. The old Serbian community from Austro-Hungary and the new Serbian community from Yugoslavia each had their own orthodox church and politics. The early Poles from the northern fishing villages, the "kashubs," once had their own village on Jones Island and didn't have much to say to the southern Poles who came later. So Frankie Yankovic didn't displace all these peoples and their musics so much as define a public space for himself and the less traditionally minded.

My last morning in Milwaukee, D. P. drove me out to visit with Louie Bashell, the "Silk Umbrella Man," generally acknowledged to be the top Slovenian-American stylist in Milwaukee. It didn't take long to find his nice, new house in the suburbs, and even less time to get settled into a pleasant and efficient interview. The basic outline of his life was quickly established. Louie was born on July 1, 1914, the same day his father opened a tavern in a mostly German neighborhood. His father played the button box or semi-tone accordion occasionally for back-of-the-bar entertainment and started Louie playing at age seven. He switched to the chromatic accordion at age twelve, took lessons from Tony Martinsek, moved to the piano accordion at fifteen, and has been "playing out for public" ever since. He went to trade school in the early thirties to be a plumber but couldn't find work when he graduated in the middle of the Depression, so he spent more time on music and worked when he could at the packing house. He married in 1940, did plumbing in the war factories, put his savings into properties, and with the help of his first and only hit record, the "Silk Umbrella Polka," in 1946, "I haven't worked in a shop since that year."

CK: *Was "Silk Umbrella Polka" a big hit in Cleveland?*
LB: Well, only like a folksong. It had Slovenian melody and Slovenian words, so all the Cleveland bands recorded it at one time or another. But it wasn't like Frankie Yankovic's impact here at all. In fact, I've never played in Cleveland. And I have an uncle with a tavern there, who hires bands, too. No, you see Milwaukee's music is not like any other. It's slower. Cleveland is going twice as fast! Milwaukee is more relaxed. People set no pace, they just live it out and enjoy as much as they can that way. No rush to get nowhere.
CK: *And your music fits that feeling?*
LB: Yes, I think so. It's really a surprising thing about Milwaukee; the Slovenian population is rather small, but it's the most popular ethnic music in Milwaukee. The Germans or the Poles may start a band, but it will be 90 percent Slovenian music.
CK: *That's the puzzle I've been working on. Why do you think that is?*
LB: It's a very melodious music. Simple music and melodious; you don't have to be a genius to play it, you know, or have good technique, or anything like that. It's just a flowing music. Polish music has various frills and trills in it. Polish music to me has a very distinct flavor. While Slovenian music is plain, simply notes that just move—nothing fancy. I've never come across a piece of Slovenian music that was difficult. The Slo-

Slovenian Style in Milwaukee 51

venians are so easily pleased. They don't have to have nothing special. The way I can see it, the Slovenians haven't got great composers or great writers, at least, I don't know about them, I don't think the world knows much about them, Slovenian opera singers or conductors....

CK: *You should have heard this paper about all the Slovenian contributions this past weekend at the conference I came out here for—the first opera house in Cleveland was a Slovenian opera house....*

LB: Yes. Yes, I'm sure....

CK: *But Slovenians really excel in straightforward simple songs?*

LB: That's right. That's my thought exactly.

CK: *And so those songs dominate in Milwaukee. The places I've been, aside from Veteran's Park, that's all I hear is Slovenian style, like at the Blue Canary, I heard Gentleman Jim for a few sets—Slovenian and country, Slovenian and country. Is that fairly typical?*

LB: Yes, I'd say so. Gentleman Jim, he's Polish by nationality, but he plays a lot of Slovenian music. It's a real odd thing that Milwaukee with so much Polish ethnic stuff around here—they have Polish schools, great Polish churches, music stores, and everything—and I have yet to see or hear an organized Polish band play Polish-type music in Milwaukee like Eddie Blazonczyk in Chicago or Walt Solek and Wojnarowski from Connecticut. But you can't get a group like that in Milwaukee to make music; they'll come right to the accordion and play Slovenian music.

CK: *Why is that?*

LB: I don't know, really. You think you'll find the answer, huh?

CK: *It probably has to do with politics, the schools, a lot of German influence....*

LB: I think it all exploded from Yankovic. When he came

to town and his music became popular—"Just Because," "Blue Skirt Waltz"—then everything else fell in place for him such as all the Slovenian songs he sang, Slovenian lyrics even on records. That was a very big impact.

CK: *But Frankie didn't push the Polish style out of Cleveland; how did he do it in Milwaukee?*

LB: He had a lot of Slovenian support here. He was not adopted by the Germans or anything like that. You see, they needed a hero back then, like Vinton is a hero to the Poles now, they were proud of him for representing them.

I remember in the late forties there was a big promotion in the Milwaukee Auditorium, eight or ten bands, Lawrence Duchow, Six Fat Dutchmen, Sammy Madden, Yankovic, my band, and some others. Frankie was crowned polka king and I was crowned Number Two. I was satisfied. And I've been holding my own here in Milwaukee; we're in the top position for 15 or 20 years now.

The reason for my longevity is that we play all kinds of music. The banjo doubles guitar and the bass doubles tuba. So I can take and play German music almost their style. And then I can play Polish music—I don't play fast enough to play Polish music like the real Polish people do. I play it actually in my own feelings. I was honored a few months ago when a lady from Europe thanked me for the finest tempo she had ever danced an oberek to. I just pick up the Polish songs by ear, kids have had them for lessons, Lush's "Hey Cavalier" I use. It all depends where I am playing, some places no polkas at all, other places, like German parties or New Year's we won't play much Polish.

CK: *Aren't there German bands for the German parties?*

LB: Oh, yeah, Johnny Hoffman, Johnny Walters, they have the German flavor, but it is still basically Slovenian music. The two accordions.

CK: *Were there always two accordions?*
LB: No, before the war it was usually a solo accordion, you know. Martinsek alone always had fifty to a hundred students, or just a trio of accordion, drums, sax. My very first records were like that; maybe my wife can find one.
CK: *I hope so. I'd like to hear it. You made other records after those, right?*
LB: Oh, yes. One just before the strike and the ban on recording. RCA hired us and later I did a few albums and 45s for them in the fifties but RCA dropped us when rock came in and then I was with Mercury a few years. The last record, about ten years ago, was with the King label in Cincinnati with all the other leaders, but the guy who hired us for that was fired soon after. It must have been a big flop.
CK: *You don't go to a studio and make records of your own?*
LB: No. There is no way to distribute them except off the bandstand. And I always say, I come to sell music, not records.
CK: *And you don't need the records to keep the band busy?*
LB: We work four nights every week and I could have stopped years ago on the income from the properties. Wednesday we're at Music Land, Sunday at the Blue Canary and Friday and Saturday are always booked ahead. My wife hasn't had me home on a Saturday in so many years we lost count.
CK: *With so much work the personnel must stay the same.*
LB: Some come and go and come back again. My fill accordion player left in '61 or '62 and then I took him back after ten years. The drummers come and go and I need substitutes; unless they do vocals they get bored 'cause I try to use the least amount of cymbals and half the banjo rhythm section, just the off beat. I insist upon

that; that's the flavor I want and that's the flavor that the people are buying for fifty years, two beat. Solid. No frills on the drums, nothin' fancy. Bass drum and sock cymbal, that's all a man has to do for me on that stage.

CK: *Do you rehearse regularly to get the sound you want, break in substitutes?*

LB: We've never had a rehearsal. Never. Except when we were doing records, of course.

CK: *Never. So the style and the book for all the bands must be pretty standard.*

LB: If you are rehearsing a lot, you start playing for the musicians. I play what the people ask for, what they remember. I play for the people 'cause they pay the freight. And there are bands that try to play just like I do, and bands with musicians who used to play with me. The country and western songs are standard, the old ones, not many modern ones, mostly Eddy Arnold, Gene Autry, "Cheatin' Heart," "Jealous Heart," "Never Ending Love." The men all have a lot of experience so really there's no problem with a request. A guy asks for "Moonlight and Roses" we play it. I play "Sweethearts on Parade" they give me an ovation. They remember.

CK: *Who are the musicians? I mean, are they all Slovenian and Polish and what do they do aside from the band?*

LB: I'm the only Slovene in the band. Let's see, Johnny Bello is Hungarian and he's over at the County Hospital. Matusek, the drummer, he's Polish, does some vocals, he's a food inspector, dairies, cheeses; Bruski, the bass, is Bohemian and sometimes he can't play during the week because he's a vice principal and has to be up for school; Robert Zir is German and he's a foreman at a chemical leather company.

CK: *So you all know each other's music in Milwaukee.*

LB: Like I said, we keep it simple and solid. For the danc-

Slovenian Style in Milwaukee

ers. You need a good partner. My wife tells me when I play bad. If she has a hard time dancing, she'll tell me something is wrong.

Mrs. Bashell was standing at my shoulder with a small pile of 78 records taken from a hiding place. "You see, Louis would just give them away if somebody asked, so I've kept them safe." We spent some time listening to records. Louie's first records, just the trio, were much wilder than I'd expected; lilting alto sax and a very busy drummer kicking things along with breaks and fills that reminded me of Chicago Dixieland—the Austin High gang, Gene Krupa or George Wettling mixing it up on the tubs. A little later, a 78 by the legendary Romy Gosz, suggested more answers than I had questions. Romy's buttery tone, vibrato, loose surging phrases, took me completely by surprise. If you played that next to a Bix Beiderbecke record, what conclusions could be drawn? Was that polka clarinetist Frank Teschmaker's musical nephew or his grandfather reincarnated? Before I could begin to sort out the German contribution to jazz from the jazz contribution to polka, we were moving along to Louis's LPs of the 1950s which seemed to get smoother and mellower with the years. They were still mostly two-beat, but the Yankovic influence was unmistakable and the net effect was of ever increasing respectability.

Within the Milwaukee Slovenian community there is some feeling that the Cleveland style became dominant just because the Slovenian community there was better off, better organized, coming from the supposedly better part of Slovenia, Steiermark,[4] while in Milwaukee more people were from Kreinmark, "lower Slovenia," and struggling with factionalism. According to this view, Cleveland has six or eight Slovenian Homes while Milwaukee's community could barely organize one and finally had to hire a Swede to manage it because the jealousies were so fierce. In the good old days there used to be regular two-by-four fights whenever a Krein walked into a

Steier tavern, but in recent decades the fisticuffs have simmered down to gossip, backbiting, and the hope that such old feuds are a stain on the Slovenian heritage that will one day fade away completely. This Steier versus Krein factionalism, however, seems to fit with my initial hunch that the Slovenian style represented a compromise or mediation between Germans and Poles; the Steiers come from the area closer to Germany and Austria and it is German values, German business sense, that they hold over the Kreins. Yet it is the Kreins who seem to make most of the music, probably, if other class/ethnic nexuses of musical creation are any guide, in an effort to transcend Steier standards and stereotypes.

Could it have been this class antagonism within the small Slovenian community of Milwaukee (and/or a lack of it in Cleveland) that somehow contributed to the hegemony of Slovenian style? One notices, in just a few days of research, that the class splits in the ethnic groups seem to go deeper in Milwaukee and are more easily acknowledged. Could this have anything to do with the long history of socialist city government as a context for ethnic identities? A lack of conventional ward politics and the usual ethnic alliances that mute class differences? A clearer ideological climate for identifying class interests and acting upon them? Or is Milwaukee's mosaic better viewed as a series of historical accidents and particulars? Poles called "Kashubs" happened to settle in one area; there happened to be enough Serbs immigrating at two different times to form two factions; for reasons best known to themselves the Slovenes from Štajerska and the Slovenes from Krajnska could never build a home big enough for both.

Along these lines, one might retitle this essay "Milwaukee: The City Where Frankie Yankovic Happened to Be Most Successful," or "It's Krein Time Again: The Poles Learn Country and Slovenian." The very special particularities of style formation in Milwaukee need more than a few days research but the few summary generalizations, both major and minor, one can make from even so swift an overview are solid enough and supportable by parallel data from other cities in the industrial heartland of America.

1. Successful proletarian styles are often ethnic hybrids. Slovenian-American polka style is an especially nice example because of its black foundation and white country adaptation, both factors personified in the banjo player who doubles on guitar.

2. Within working class culture, there is a tendency toward localized ethnic hegemony. A streamlined Slovenian-American style wins out in Milwaukee. But in Pittsburgh there are young bands like the Treltones of Slovakian and German backgrounds who sing exclusively in Polish and play the Polish-American "Chicago" or "honky" style made popular by Lil' Wally. The main polka clubs in Pittsburgh are only about 50 percent Polish with a lot of Slovakian, Irish, and Italian members. New York City is the only place where the old-fashioned Eastern style of Polish-American polkas still holds sway and the leading band is the pet project of an Irish-American banker. In Buffalo, polkas are maintained almost exclusively by a small core of fans within the Polish-American community. In industrial Massachusetts and the Connecticut Valley area, Happy Louis Dessault's distinct variation on "honky" style is the norm and a number of other bands have French-Canadian members who sing and play the Polish way. So each locality is different but one ethnic style tends to dominate, usually a Polish one.

3. A minor point perhaps, but the leading stylists are often prophets without special honor in their own cities, witness Yankovic big in Milwaukee and taken for granted in Cleveland. The best Buffalo bands draw much bigger crowds and better money on the road, and the big name Chicago groups report the same pattern.

4. A few of the older bands in Milwaukee and in each other locality feel the pull of respectable culture as they tend to become two-beat "society bands" or what the timeworn label in Buffalo calls a "radio-recording orchestra." The transition

from people's "polka hop" to "businessman's bounce" is easily made if you want to, a shift from one restricted code in Bernstein's sense[5] to a still more restricted one perhaps.

5. Because the local style is ethnic and working class it is also community and family centered and supported. This means that musicians and fans in one localized ethclass, say Slovenes in Milwaukee, don't know or care what the musicians and fans in another localized ethclass, say the Poles in Chicago, are doing, and vice versa. There is surprisingly little communication between the Slovenian, Polish, and Czech-Bohemian polka traditions over the past century or so of development in the new world, and no communication at all between these Slavic styles of the Northeast to Midwest and the flourishing polka traditions of the Mexican-American and Native American communities in the Southwest that have also been evolving for 120 years. That all these different segments of the working class have been dancing to the same beat for so long without being aware of each other is surely a fact worth thinking about.

6. And what is an appropriate conclusion to draw from this material for a conference on "folk music and modern sound?" I have argued elsewhere that the "folk" concept is a dangerous mystification, especially when it is used to folk over the working class.[6] And I'm not very happy with "modern sound" to designate what "folk" evolves into, since its denotive center is amorphous and the connotations of slick, commercial, alienated, mass mediated, all the heavier. Yet I have a good idea of what the conference title is trying to put a finger on and I'm sure that the Frankie Yankovic example is as much at the heart of it as B. B. King's guitar style. Why not just talk about people's music, or the working people's music that's not dependent on state subsidy or corporate mediation, and then celebrate the fact that it changes in striking ways from old country to new, from rural to urban settings, from one city to another, and from generation to generation.

[1] Norbert Blei, "The Long, Lusty Reign of Franky the First," *Chicago Tribune Magazine*, April 13, 1971, 42.

[2] "In Pursuit of Polka Happiness," Charles and A. Keil, *Cultural Correspondence*, No. 5, 1977.

[3] Charles Keil, *Tiv Song* (Chicago: University of Chicago Press, 1979), 6-7.

[4] I've kept the German or English spelling for these terms because these areas, Steiermark and Kreinmark, were under Austro-Hungarian control during the period when most Slovenes emigrated to Milwaukee bringing their sectional rivalries with them. Today these areas are called Štajerška and Krajnskã.

[5] See Mary Douglas's insightful short summary of Bernstein's work in her *Implicit Meanings: Essays in Anthropology* (London and Boston: Routledge & Kegan Paul Ltd., 1975), 173-180.

[6] Charles Keil, "Who Needs 'the Folk'?" *Journal of the Folklore Institute* (Indiana University), 15 (1978), 263-265; "Comment: The Concept of 'the Folk'," *Journal of the Folklore Institute*, 16 (1979), 209-210.

Ethnic and Popular Style in America

Richard Spottswood

IT IS GOOD to note that the seventies have brought about an enlargement of the arena devoted to the study and discussion of American popular and folk music to include the current and historic activities of ethnic minority elements of our society. The survey of what, for want of a better term, is called "ethnic" music has already begun to prove particularly rewarding, as is evidenced by the fine work being done by scholars like Mark Slobin and Charlie Keil.

My own interest in ethnic music evolved while I was in the process of editing and selecting materials for the Library of Congress record series, Folk Music in America, beginning in 1974. I knew from the start that I wanted to obtain and use some folk-styled performances from non-English-speaking cultures, but I had little notion of where to begin or what sort of music would prove aesthetically rewarding as well as being useful documentation. But I only needed to scratch the surface to find that the same stalwart record companies who had immortalized Jimmie Rodgers, the Skillet Lickers, and Bessie Smith had, with equal vigor, tapped the roots of vital folk and popular music cultures from nearly every ethnic group in America. What's more, they had been doing it practically since the birth of the commercial recording industry in the 1890s. And it took only a little further surface scratching to discover that some of that music can still be heard today often in the environs in which it flourished then, side by side with music which reflects internal musical developments, and varying degrees of accommodation with American popular styles, such as rock and country and western.

Much work awaits those willing to explore the field to track down ethnic music in contemporary settings. Most of us are familiar with the current Irish revival; the Cajun music of Louisiana and the Norteño music of Texas are both flourishing in the post-McLuhan age, successfully defying those forces which seek to incorporate their distinctive features into the musical melting pot. In part, these musical cultures are thriving because of reinforcement from the outside. Significant numbers of Americans outside these musical cultures are supporting them by record purchases, sponsoring concerts in remote locales and even learning to play the music themselves.

With somewhat less attention, other European-American groups are also holding their own. There is a fine Ukrainian Hutsul group who is keeping Carpathian mountain music alive in Philadelphia. Several Polish highlander groups in Chicago actively support the archaic fiddling and singing styles of the Tatra Mountains, which coexist happily alongside the big-time polka outfits of Marion Lush and Eddie Blazonczyk. Old and new Greek, Turkish, and Armenian styles can be found in the urban centers of both coasts.

Getting at the roots of ethnic music is a formidable challenge. Newspapers, printed music, pamphlets and other ephemera will yield much to one who is willing to explore them. But the most important and reliable source is sound recordings themselves, primary documents which need to be collected, reissued, organized, and discussed, so that we may gain some insights into the history and development of individual ethnic styles.

For my own part, I am gathering raw data from the files of the Columbia, Victor, Edison, Decca, Brunswick, and Gennett companies to assemble a discographic work which will identify every known recording made by these and other companies for ethnic groups through 1942. Recording dates, locations, vocal and instrumental details, composer and artists credits, master numbers, and release data will comprise the basic elements for artists of each nationality. Old recording ledgers, catalogs, file cards, and label coupling sheets still in company files are the primary sources. Occasionally, copies of the records themselves are available for examination and audition.

I would like to give a brief idea of some of the components which make up what we call ethnic music, a term, incidentally, which has not usually been applied to this music in the past. It is not easy to give an all encompassing description, since its boundaries often overlap with country, art, and pop music. Great cantors, like Pierre Pinchik and Joseph Rosenblatt, found their records issued in both Victor's Jewish and classical "Red Seal" series. Popular Polish, Italian, or Greek singers frequently covered pop hits in their own languages. Occasionally it worked the other way around: the great Mississippi fiddle and guitar team of Willie Narmour and Shell Smith made Okeh records which were retitled, recredited, and issued in Okeh's Mexican series. Bradley Kincaid's clear Kentucky tenor can be heard on several Bluebird Irish releases. A number of West Indian recordings were released in the popular, race, and even Spanish catalogs.

Even between various ethnic music catalogs a single recording could be employed more than once. Polkas, schottisches, and waltzes had (and still have) an appeal which crosses Scandinavian, Slavic, Anglo, American Indian, and Hispanic musical cultures. A popular recording by the German-descended bandleader "Whoopee John" Wilfahrt of New Ulm, Minnesota, could be found in the German, Polish, Mexican, Lithuanian, and even American hillbilly series. Abe Schwartz, a superior Jewish fiddler, orchestra and recording director, also saw his Yiddish dance tunes retitled for the Rumanian, Greek, and even Spanish lists. I don't mean to imply that melodies, dances, and instrumental styles weren't shared across linguistic and geographic boundaries before the record-making process. They were, but my guess is that record distribution has had much to do with musical cross-pollenization in America during this century. As you might expect, the greatest body of non-English recording activity in America has been in Spanish, which is, after all, the dominant language of this hemisphere. Spanish-language music was actively exploited from the first. And by 1910, material recorded in New York as well as below the border was appearing regularly on the Victor, Columbia, and Edison labels. Field trips with portable recording equipment were regularly undertaken to Port-of-Spain, Mexico City, Havana, Bogota, and other Central and South American urban centers long before blues and country music were captured on location in this country. One reason for this extensive early activity was that portable crank-wound record players could be used anywhere, unlike other products of the emerging American technology which required an external power source. And records effectively promoted the sale of phonographs everywhere.

The Spanish lists are extensive, and, more than any other series, reflect the growth and development of our own popular music in this century. The catalogs show music whose scope is Pan-American, and other music of distinctly national or regional character. At first, all recording activity in the Americas was undertaken by North American companies. Later on, subsidiaries of these companies were established in larger countries like Brazil and Mexico, and independent companies were born alongside them. By the 1920s, the Pan-American market was organized to the extent that North American companies no longer needed field trips beyond the Caribbean region, and records made in each of the Americas were routinely offered for sale in the others. My discography will only account for a selected number of U.S.-made Spanish-language records, since limitations of time and space preclude a survey of the entire corpus. Still, that section of the discography will be by far the largest, and a survey of the whole is well worth undertaking. Latin music of all kinds has regularly crossed over into our own domain. The rhumba bands of Xavier Cugat and Desi Arnaz, the mambo outfits of Perez Prodo and Miguelito Valdez, classical performers like the tenor Emilio de Gogorza and pianist Jose Iturbi are among the well-known performers. Popular songs from below the border, like "Amapola," "La Cucaracha," "El Manicero" (The Peanut Vendor), and "The Girl from Impanema" are as well known to us as "Stardust" and "Don't Be Cruel."

One surprising feature of the Hispanic lists is the amount of folk-derived material even on early recordings. The Cuarteto Coculense of Mexico featured an authentic country fiddler. Ramon Garcia ("El Gaitero") sang in the Asturian style, accompanied by his own bagpipes. Several singers and singing groups performed traditional and topical material with their own stringed instrument accompaniments. These records could be found regularly in the Mexican, Cuban, and Puerto Rican catalogs after 1905, years before we could enjoy comparable material from the Appalachian and rural black sectors of our own society. By the 1920s, when field recording units regularly visited southern cities, their stops included San Antonio and El Paso. Here they gathered the Norteño music of the Texas border country for the first time.

In contrast, music from European-Americans filtered into American studies more slowly. A few German, French, and Polish performers were recorded in the 1890s, and Jewish, Scandinavian, and Hungarian artists followed them early in this century. But the need for American-produced records in European languages was not so immediate.

Recording centers in London, Paris, Milan, St. Petersburg, and other European cities were established before 1905, and connections with U. S. firms meant that music from imported sources could be reissued here inexpensively in quantity. The outbreak of the World War meant that masters could no longer be shipped from European ports and that overseas recording activity was itself cut back drastically. American companies began to increase foreign language recording activity in 1915, with Columbia even sending a field unit to Chicago especially to record ethnic music there. By 1916, domestic ethnic production was in high gear; new songs and music reflected various blends of European style tempered with the new American experience. Patriotic songs were being churned out by Tin Pan Alley for record and sheet music consumption during those feverish years. Ethnic artists were not far behind in their output of songs reflecting sentiment for a troubled mother country or words of encouragement for American troops, following our joining the battle in 1917. Indeed, right up to the eve of our entry, record companies were even producing German patriotic material—a good example of the studied neutrality of profit making.

In the years following the armistice, foreign-made recordings were again employed, but these merely augmented productions by domestic artists who were now familiar as record makers, whose recording incomes and reputations augmented what they were able to earn on the concert or music-hall stages in their communities. They were by now popular presences to foreign-born Americans, and new recordings by Morris Goldstein, Olle I Skrathult, Gennaro Amato, and Ignacy Ulatowski were consistently well received. These singers and countless others usually recorded with musicians regularly employed by the record companies in house ensembles. These musicians could read quickly, accompany singers with minimal rehearsal time, and complete a session of four songs or so in one and a half to two hours. They knew their craft well, and were trained by experience in the limited dynamics of the early recording process, but their accompaniments and arrangements were standardized and predictable, giving a numbing similarity to most of their records. Still, house musicians couldn't handle everything, and even the early postwar years produced an occasional Polish folk fiddler or accordion player, an Italian zampogna (bagpipe) group, or exciting Greek singing with native musicians.

The production of folk and folk-derived music expanded during the 1920s, especially after electrical recording was introduced successfully in 1925. By then there was a demonstrated demand for music directly from the village and rural roots which reflected the backgrounds of millions of immigrants. These were the same years which saw the beginnings of recorded blues and country music, suggesting a new acceptance for the less formal styles of all American minorities. One excellent musician who first found himself on records in December 1925 was the Ukrainian-born fiddler Pawlo (Paul) Humeniuk, who was born in Galicia in 1884 and emigrated to America some time before 1909. His Columbia records of polkas, kolomyikas, and kozaks were immediately successful, and early in 1926, he assembled a small case of singers, actors, and musicians to produce a two-sided, twelve-inch record of a skit called simply "Ukrainian Wedding." From the dialogue to the fiddle tunes, and excerpts of wedding songs complete with the loud wailing of the bride, it was a convincing vignette of a village wedding in the old country and a runaway hit, even when twelve-inch records were selling for $1.25. Its appeal spread to other national groups, and recordings of wedding scenes and other ceremonial and holiday activities were being turned out as fast as they could be produced. I'm not sure what connection there might be between the "Ukrainian Wedding" and a successful Columbia release the following year (1927) of "A Corn Licker Still in Georgia" by the Skillet Lickers, but the latter follows the same pattern of loosely knit dialogue interspersed with songs and fiddle tunes. It was also a runaway hit which engendered many sequels and imitations in the growing country music market. It is arguable that one consciously suggested the other to some recording executive, or even that emerging radio drama prompted them both.

While on the subject of hits, I should mention another development in the 1920s which proved to be a lasting trend—non-English recordings of American hit songs for other national groups. "Yes, We Have No Bananas," a 1921 success which made fun of the language difficulties of an Italian fruit vendor, was covered in Yiddish, Polish, and ironically, even Italian. "Barney Google" and "Mr. Gallagher and Mr. Shean" were covered soon after, and the race was on. By 1928, Victor could boast in the trade journal *Talking Machine World* that the song "Ramona" had been recorded by them in ten languages. This activity continues even today. Country songs, for instance, are sung in Ukrainian in Canada, in Acadian French in Louisiana, or in Polish by the polka bands of Chicago and New England.

The record industry began to go through some hard times during the mid-1920s. Radio's improved sound expedited the development of electrical recording techniques, but there was no getting away from the fact that its entertainment was provided in more varied and extended formats, and at no direct cost to its public. But, with the exception of country music, radio provided little direct appeal to minority audiences. This is not to say that there was no ethnic programming during the 1920s, but such fare was infrequently and irregularly scheduled, and usually inaccessible to audiences beyond the largest cities. Ethnic record sales, therefore, managed to hold their own, and continued to appear at a growing rate through 1930, as the companies placed greater reliance on minority groups. Folk-derived performances abounded, and the years from 1925-1930 may properly be considered a "golden era," just as others consider this era an important period of blues, jazz, and country recording. For example, I refer again to the Folk Music in America series which contains traditionally grounded music from Finnish, West Indian, Irish, Polish, Jewish, Greek, Lithuanian, Spanish, and other sources, much of it from these fruitful years.

By 1930 several factors combined to curtail ethnic and other minority recording activity. The Depression decreased the amount of money available for entertainment. And, by this time, immigrants who had arrived before the Emergency Quota Act in 1921 (which reduced the flood of immigration to a trickle) were becoming assimilated by varying degrees into the "melting pot" and increasingly able to enjoy popular radio entertainment and the new talking pictures along with English-speaking Americans. Radio was free and the movies cost only twenty-five cents, but records still retailed for seventy-five cents, a price maintained throughout the Depression. Smaller ethnic series were discontinued entirely; others began to rely again on imported masters or cut down severely on new releases. Some ethnic groups must have felt the financial strain less severely than others, if record production is any barometer. Records in Greek, Polish, and Italian were still actively released throughout the worst years, while records in German, the Scandinavian tongues, and in the Irish series were curtailed.

Production didn't really pick up again until the late 1930s, following the proliferation of juke boxes in the taverns and bars which formed an important element of community social life. The polka bands of various nationalities which had emerged in the 1920s continued to be popular in the 1930s, but with the release of Will Glahe's Victor recording of "Beer Barrel Polka" around 1937, the juke boxes and polka bands enjoyed a new boom era. The Glahe record was released on a new Victor "International Novelties" series, tailored especially for the juke box trade. Other companies quickly followed suit, and the records managed to find audiences among many national groups, which meant that larger sales could be expected from fewer releases and that profits would increase accordingly. Prominent ethnic bandleaders altered and denationalized their names: Abe Ellstein became Leon Stenier, Edmund Terlikowski became Eddie Terley, Wasyl Gula became Bill Gale as they and others sought to disguise their origins and broaden their appeal. It worked, and the polka bands enjoyed a following they haven't lost to this day. But this was mass market music compared to what had gone before; more distinctive styles and traditions were rapidly losing favor. The ethnic catalogs remained but, except for an occasional reissue of an earlier success, the music began to vary less from one series to another, drawing inspiration from either the generalized polka boom or Tin Pan Alley. World War II put another heavy crimp into record production, and, by 1952, the large companies brought production of ethnic music to a virtual halt.

But by this time, smaller companies had taken up much of the slack. Some custom ethnic label activity existed even during the 1920s, but it never competed significantly with major labels, and it did not continue into the Depression. But in the early 1930s, an ambitious multitalented singer and producer named Tetos Demetriades discovered a new wrinkle. He was a competent and popular Greek tenor who had recorded light music prolifically during the 1920s, and had begun assuming some administrative duties in Victor's Foreign Records Department. These led to Demetriades's own Orthophonic label, whose products carried the official Nipper trademark, were mastered and pressed by Victor, and advertised prominently in the company's foreign catalogs. Orthophonic offered records in Greek, Turkish, and Albanian at least through the war years, and Demetriades's success enabled him to begin a second label, Standard, which offered more general fare and is still active today. Other independent ethnic companies followed Standard and Orthophonic, particularly after 1945, as relatively inexpensive tape mastering became possible and as record processing plants became available in most major cities. Polkas were still big business, and many independents still followed these trends closely. But smaller overhead requirements meant that diversity was again possible, and specialized Serbian, Hungarian, Irish, and Polish labels have been capable of turning out some exciting music. They continue to serve as documents of both tradition and change, revealing a combined pride in both Americanization and in the distinctive facets of each ethnic community's cultural heritage.

Study and collecting in the ethnic arena is way overdue, which means that the records are scarcer than they would have been a few years ago. We have been remiss over the years in ignoring contributions from non-English-speaking cultures in our midst. Their music was not recorded in the field to any significant degree nor was it dealt with extensively in the journals. If this paper seems to document recordings more than music, it is because they seem today to be the only meaningful access to this music of the past. Much of it has yet to be heard, let alone studied, reissued, and related to contemporary musical expression. Certainly ethnic is an integral part of the "modern sound" of the twentieth century, having drawn from and contributed to American popular music. Just as Yiddish audiences delighted in the modified "Mr. Gallagher and Mr. Shean," so the rest of us have adopted the Yiddish "Bel Mir Bist Du Schoen," the Mexican "La Cucaracha," the calypsonian "Rum and Coca-Cola," and the Polish "Clarinet Polka" into our own collective musical consciousness. These days, conscientious folk festival producers are trying to locate good ethnic performers to add to the usual Anglo-black mixture. Reissues of important historical recordings are beginning to appear, and current artists like Clifton Chenier, Lydia Mendoza, and Eddie Blazonczyk are attracting audiences far beyond the boundaries of their original communities. I hope the process will continue; we will be all the richer for it.

PART III

The Religious Sound

New Directions in Sacred Harp Singing

Doris J. Dyen

I WANT TO SHARE with you some thoughts I have had on the subject of recent developments in Sacred Harp singing, and to invite comments and discussion on new trends that I perceive in this constellation of folk music traditions. I am particularly concerned with the relationship of Sacred Harp singing both to the mass media and to the scholars and fieldworkers who have been endeavoring to document the music for research. The aims of scholars and the aims of media specialists are different from each other: scholars want mainly to document traditions and preserve them for present and future study; media specialists want to produce well-crafted recordings, videotapes, films, etc., for presentation to the public (sometimes with an eye to possible commercial viability). Both groups are well-meaning in their efforts (sometimes the same person is both scholar and media specialist), and usually want to have the best interests of the performers at heart; yet both these groups of outsiders have an enormous impact on the performers they work with. This problem is compounded when the scholar or specialist is also involved in public programming, for then that person's own visibility is greater and his or her financial backing, coming directly from the government, carries more weight and influence.

Recorded documentation in sound of Sacred Harp music

began in the 1930s and has continued ever since. The most extensive recording efforts have involved white singers who sing from the Denson revision of the *Sacred Harp* book (first published in 1936 as *The Original Sacred Harp*, revised by Paine Denson from Benjamin Franklin White's *Sacred Harp*, 1869 edition), who are concentrated mainly in north and central Alabama, Georgia, and areas of Tennessee and Mississippi. So widespread has been the dissemination of the Denson singers' performance via these recordings that, for much of the outside world, their style *is* Sacred Harp singing.

The emphasis by outside fieldworkers and recording companies (such organizations as the Library of Congress and Folkways Records) on the Denson tradition has fueled the disagreements over style and repertory which already had existed to some extent between singers from the Denson revision and those who use the W. M. Cooper revision of the *Sacred Harp* (first published in 1902 as *The B. F. White Sacred Harp*, revised by Cooper from B. F. White's 1869 edition of the *Sacred Harp*). The Cooper-book adherents are concentrated mainly in southern Alabama, and in Florida, with some singers in other areas of the Deep South. Outside workers have in effect given a stamp of approval to one branch of the tradition, while assigning a secondary status to all others. Furthermore, it is not the intrinsic value of one or another branch which has determined the situation, but the weight of historical accident: the Denson-book singers were the ones recorded earliest and most heavily.

But there have also been stylistic changes brought about in the white Sacred Harp singers' performance, due to increased public exposure. One result of the interest by fieldworkers in recording and rerecording these singers has been that the singers themselves have become interested in producing their own recordings. Both the Cooper-book and the Denson-book singers have done this on local labels. The Denson singers in particular have been trying for a more blended, "refined" choral sound—because they have had more opportunities to hear recordings of themselves, and because they have been hearing comments on their music from the fieldworkers.

In the last ten years, singers from the Denson tradition have had the opportunity to do fieldwork of their own. Many of them have been invited to perform at festivals and at events on northern college campuses, such as the annual sing of the newly formed New England Sacred Harp convention. Even the Cooper-book singers, though more isolated, have obtained recordings of college groups and pop singers singing Sacred Harp songs. I had the odd experience myself of having an informant in south Alabama play for me a selection from a recording of Sacred Harp music done by the American Music Group (a University of Illinois performing ensemble)—a recording in which I had sung.

When these singers participate in outside events or listen to outsiders' recordings of the music, it cannot help but have an effect on their own singing styles and repertory, since the interests, singing style, and background of the outsiders are not like the singers' own. College-student enthusiasts request songs that the singers might not traditionally sing at home. When singing schools are held as part of these demonstrations, the invited singers must scale down the traditional two-week school to two days or even one morning; to do this, they have had to develop ways of presenting the singing-school material in a much different and more abbreviated form, and for a much different sort of "class," from the ones they are used to. More important, these traveling singer/demonstrators begin to perceive these new methods of presentation as being desirable and worthwhile changes and additions to their tradition, because of the outside public exposure generated. Outside influence has thus brought about changes of format and repertory in the tradition, as well as the changes in attitude.

The effect of outside influence has been noticeable also— and perhaps even more strongly felt—on black Sacred Harp singers in southeast Alabama. These people, who use the Cooper edition of the book, as do the white singers in that area, began to be studied and recorded in the late 1930s, the most notable early researcher being John W. Work. In the mid-1930s, the black community in the area had published its own four-shape-note book, *The Colored Sacred Harp* (Ozark, Alabama, 1934, Judge Jackson, author). Due to internal dissent among the singers, and stylistic peculiarities in the book, *The Colored Sacred Harp* was never accepted fully in its own community; for years, numerous copies lay unused in the home of the book's compiler, Judge Jackson. One steady, though small, market for the book, however, was scholars from colleges and institutions. So knowledge of black Sacred Harp singing, at least in written form, remained available to the outside world.

During the 1950s and 1960s various members of the black singing community in southeast Alabama began to try to promote Sacred Harp singing among other black people in the Ozark-Dothan area, and to raise money. They turned to the most easily available local media, and established first their own regular radio and later television programs of Sacred Harp singing. Only a few singers could fit into the studio at any one time, and these singers had to sing standing up, not seated; so a small change had entered the tradition.

In the late 1960s, scholars began to rediscover the black tradition as a living performance style of shape-note singing, and came into the area to do biographical interviewing of the singers and to make field recordings of the sings. (The main scholars involved at this time were Joe Dan Boyd and William Tallmadge.) About 1970, the black community was asked to send a group of singers to Washington, D.C., to attend the Smithsonian Festival of American Folklife. That same year, a group of white Sacred Harpers from the north Alabama Denson tradition came to the Smithsonian Festival as well.

Because of this meeting in Washington, the black singers acquired knowledge of other Sacred Harp styles that they had previously not known about, and acquired new goals and attitudes about their own tradition. They realized that *The*

Colored Sacred Harp book was of great interest to the outside world and decided to try to reprint it, which they did in 1973 with financial backing from the Alabama Council on the Arts and Humanities—even though there still was not wholehearted internal community support for the effort! These singers also decided that a good way of promoting black Sacred Harp singing would be to produce a record, particularly since they now knew that Sacred Harp groups elsewhere had been featured on commercially available recordings. They produced their own record through a small gospel-recording company in Memphis in the mid-1970s. The singers also expanded their own media exposure to include regular television appearances, again with funding from the Alabama Council on the Arts and Humanities.

Another far-reaching change in the black Sacred Harp tradition was the establishment by the singers who went on the Washington trip of a concert-performing ensemble called the Wiregrass Sacred Harp Singers. The name, taken from a plant which was formerly common in the area, was first applied to the singers when they attended the Smithsonian Festival; since then, under that name, the group has continued to give concerts as invited demonstrators for mixed audiences in Alabama and elsewhere. The ensemble exists as a supplementary organization, separate from the traditional black Sacred Harp hierarchy of county and state conventions. It does not receive its financial support from the black community through traditional means such as collections taken up at sings; instead most of its funding comes from local white patrons and from outside government sources. Within the rank and file black singing community in southeast Alabama, the Wiregrass Sacred Harp Singers is perceived as a somewhat "foreign" organization.

The singers in the Wiregrass Sacred Harp group, though drawn from the traditional singing community, adopt a different format for singing when performing as members of the Wiregrass ensemble, and do not use the traditional black

Sacred Harp style. They sing while standing, instead of sitting; they do not sing in the square formation, but use instead a chorus-style arrangement; they do not use the customary dance-like leading style which they call "walking their time," instead the leader remains still, in one place, and faces the audience not the singers; they do not rotate leaders, instead the group has a named director, Dewey P. Williams, who leads all the songs; they do not use the highly ornamented singing style normally found in black Sacred Harp singing, but sing the music fairly "straight"; and there is little of the call-and-response give and take that characterizes traditional black Sacred Harp style. For the Wiregrass Singers are not performing the music as participants in a sing with fifty to one hundred other people of their own community's social and religious milieu. Instead they are performing as a group of ten to fifteen singers who are providing concert entertainment for nonparticipating audiences of people from outside the tradition, usually on a raised stage and often under special lights and with microphone amplification.

The repertory sung by the Wiregrass Sacred Harp group is small compared to the repertory normally found in black Sacred Harp sings, and contains mainly songs which the singers feel they perform the best, and which will be most acceptable and pleasing to their concert audiences. The concerts given by the group tend to repeat the same songs, and the songs are ones which the singers identify as being the easiest or least challenging songs in their traditional repertory.

Thus, in response to outside interest and influence, a new organization has sprung up within the black Sacred Harp community, taking its place beside the ongoing traditional organizational structures. This new organization is related to the black Sacred Harp tradition in that it uses some of the same repertory and some of the same singers. But its performance structure and style, its contexts of performance, and its basic purpose, are so different from those of the black

Sacred Harp tradition that they must be regarded as major changes and additions *to* that tradition.

Audiences who see performances by the Wiregrass Sacred Harp Singers, who attend one- or two-day singing schools and other demonstrations by the white Denson-book singers for festivals or on college campuses, or who see films or hear recordings by one of the singers—these audiences are not really seeing the Sacred Harp traditions as such. They are seeing instead elements of those traditions that have been adapted to suit the audiences themselves: they are seeing media-inspired events *based* on the Sacred Harp traditions.

Both black and white Sacred Harp singers seem willing to apply their talents to changing their traditions to suit this new and eager outside public. They seem to tolerate the changes as being necessary to preserve and promote the music they care about. And such changes may or may not necessarily be detrimental to the music. But the situation poses a dilemma for scholars, media specialists, festival organizers, and others, who, by their very efforts to document a tradition, assume an active role in encouraging and even initiating changes in that tradition.

Gospel Goes Uptown:
White Gospel Music, 1945-1955

Charles K. Wolfe

IN DECEMBER 1953, *Billboard*, the leading trade publication for the commercial music industry, surveyed the status of gospel music in America, and began by explaining:

> The gospel field includes a wide variety of music—hymns, popular gospel songs, religious folk tunes bearing a close relation to spirituals and religious adaptations of pop tunes. There is an even wider variety of gospel artists. They include large groups like the Chuck Wagon Gang which has been spreading the word on Columbia records for many, many years; choruses such as the Anita Kerr singers on Decca, vocal quartets like the Blackwood Brothers on RCA Victor, the Harmoneers on Bibletone and the Stamps Quartet; duos like the Bailes Brothers on King or the Louvin Brothers on Capitol; trios like the Le Fevre Trio on Bibletone; and individual gospel singers who dedicate their careers to sacred music, and such as George Beverley Shea on RCA Victor and Martha Carson on Capitol.

The very fact that *Billboard* would even do a major story on gospel music in 1953 reflects just how far the music had come in the post-World War II years; the diversity of styles and artists mentioned reflects the music's widening appeal, and gradual movement into the mainstream of popular American music. (The entire world of black gospel music, which *Billboard* and the music world in general then referred to as "spiritual" music, was not even included in this list.) Long considered a cousin of country music, and often lumped with country music in attendance statistics and record sales, white gospel music was coming into its own in 1953. Gospel songs were not only infesting the country and western charts in 1953, but they were appearing on the pop charts and selling millions of recordings.

To appreciate how quickly gospel music had commercialized in the postwar era, one can turn to a parallel article in *Billboard* dating from a scant eight years earlier, February 10, 1945. Subtitled, "Singing groups and folios all bring in the shekels while the pubs collect," this article also surveyed the state of gospel music, but it did not mention the name of a single quartet or performer. Instead, gospel music was seen as a world dominated by clever and successful publishers, a world of publishing that was "a closed corporation" dominated by a handful of Southern publishers, and impervious to "outside" (i.e., Northern) publishers or songwriters. "The gospel music pubs are good business men. They build and supply an established and expanding market with a kind of music alien to a great segment of the U.S. which is as deeply rooted in American tradition as hot dogs and ice cream sodas. They train youngsters in giving with their tunes, spot them on radio stations where they do a terrif plug job, and collect royalty for performances from the broadcasters and plenty from the song folios they have the gospel singers sell via their airings." Publishers like the Stamps-Baxter company with three printing plants in the South were reporting sales of over 2,000,000 songbooks in 1944, while the older James D. Vaughan Company in Tennessee was claiming over 7,000,000 copies of its various books in use throughout the South. Most of the gospel quartets were "trained in music conservatories usually located in the plants" of the publishers, and "are made up of simple folk who feel that their work on the stations is not so important from a financial point of view as is the spreading of the word by song." Publications included not only biannual shape-note songbooks (using a seven-shape note system dating from an 1846 songbook published in Philadelphia by one Jesse B. Aikin and adapted by the influential singing schools in the Shenandoah Valley in the latter half of the nineteenth century) full of 75 percent new songs, but also various magazines such as Vaughan's *Family Visitor*, Stamps-Baxter's *Gospel Music News*, or Hartford's (Hot Springs, Arkansas) *The Herald*, which kept fans up on the latest singing conventions, songbooks, and the whereabouts of various company-sponsored quartets and groups. It was an economic system that dated from 1910, when James D. Vaughan got the idea to send out a quartet to publicize his new songbooks and songs, a system whereby most singing groups worked, directly or indirectly, for the publishers; the main concession to technology had been the companies' willingness to use radio as an extension of the singing convention circuit, and their willingness to sign an agreement with SESAC (one of the three major licensing companies) in 1935 to collect money from radio performances of gospel songs. Gospel music in 1945 had not yet been "professionalized," but it had been thoroughly commercialized for some time.

Yet changes were underway, and some quartets and singing groups were breaking away from the publishers' domination. One of Vaughan's quartets in Alabama headed by John Daniel went out on their own in the early 1940s and soon had a regular program on WSM that was fed over the NBC network, touring as far north as Canada and as far south as Jacksonville. Another Vaughan quartet headed by Claude Sharpe joined the Grand Ole Opry, becoming the Old Hickory Singers and winning a major label recording contract with Columbia to feature old sentimental songs and barbershop harmonies. The Speer Family, after stints with Vaughan and Stamps-Baxter, began to make a living on their own performances. Even earlier there had been isolated cases of quartets making it solely on the strength of their performances; one case was the MacDonald Brothers Quartet from Missouri, who recorded and toured extensively in the 1930s without ever signing an agreement with a publisher. The Chuck Wagon Gang from Texas attracted a huge following on the strength of their radio shows and records, but very rarely made personal appearances, and allowed Stamps-Baxter songs to dominate their repertoire. The Rangers, another Texas group, toured more extensively and during the early 1940s had two daily fifteen minute spots on CBS sponsored not by publishers of songbooks, but by the Vicks Chemical Company and B. C. Headache Powders. For all practical purposes, the Chuck Wagon Gang, the MacDonald Brothers, and the Rangers were the only white gospel groups to be heard on major record labels on the eve of the war.

The publishers exercised a number of effective controls over the quartets, and over their artistic development. In 1940, for instance, Stamps-Baxter "sponsored" 42 different quartets in different parts of the country. This sponsorship took two forms: in the most direct form, the publishing company paid for a car, travel expenses, and even salaries for quartets to travel around popularizing their songs. A less direct form allowed other singing groups to buy Stamps songbooks at a highly profitable discount if they would agree to sing out of these books exclusively, and to sell only Stamps books. Such latter groups could make their own travel expenses by selling trunkloads of the latest Stamps books at the singing conventions and church singings they attended. Publishers affected far more than what songs groups could sing, however. In one notorious case that was mediated by SESAC in the early 1940s, a publisher became upset when one of its quartets won a commercial sponsorship on a local radio station, a sponsorship from a tonic manufacturer. The company learned that the tonic contained alcohol, and, worried about its image, demanded the quartet drop the sponsor. In fact, when quartets won commercial sponsors, their shows often continued to include plugs for the songbooks they were singing from, as well as plugs for their commercial sponsor. As late as 1947 the Famous Stamps Quartet featured gospel pioneer Frank

Stamps on their transcribed radio show selling American Beauty Flour as well as the latest Stamps songbooks. "What New York pub wouldn't give his eyetooth for such an arrangement," commented *Billboard*. Finally, the publishers exercised control over the career and personal decisions of its groups. When the young Blackwood Brothers signed a sponsorship agreement with Stamps-Baxter in 1938, they were urged to drop their guitar accompaniment in favor of a pianist, since V. O. Stamps felt a gospel quartet should have a piano backing. Later, in 1940, the Stamps company urged them to move from their base in Shreveport to the distant prairies of Shenendoah, Iowa.

All of this domination was to change radically in the decade after World War II, and to change with a suddenness that was to bewilder many in the gospel music community, to embitter others, and to enrich still others. White gospel music, which had been stable throughout most of the other twentieth-century changes that shook pop, jazz, and country music, which had seemed impervious to economic and social upheavals of the day, underwent in a few years a complete revolution, and moved from being a publisher-dominated music to an artist-dominated music. By 1955 the quartets which had once been hired hands for the publishers would be buying out the floundering publishing houses; the music which had once been characterized by audience participation and group singing would become a spectator art. By 1957 Frank Stamps, about the only one of the old publishers to try to come to grips with the new age, would tell a Nashville courtroom: "Most of the quartets have quit using any gospel publishers' songs; most of them are singing spirituals now and a lot of them get them from recording school; they don't come out of our business and they don't come out of Baxter's or Vaughan's or any other southern publishers; most of the quartets, for five or six years, have been singing this other type music." During this process, the quartet music once so exclusively thought a unique feature of Southern culture gained nationwide exposure, and gospel music moved into the limelight of mainstream pop music. This paper is an attempt to explore some of the causes of this sudden change, and to identify some of the key individuals who, for better or for worse, forged a revolution in America's most conservative type of music.

One phenomenon which had a tremendous impact on gospel music was the sudden proliferation of independent record companies in the late 1940s. During the 1920s, major recording companies like Victor and Columbia had recorded many of the small, semiamateur quartets that were working throughout the South, issuing their releases in their various "country" or "old-time" series. Many of these groups recorded only two or four sides, often after promising the company to buy so many copies themselves, and thus the records were distributed only within the quartet's home base, and only garnered sales of from 3,000 to 5,000. (A handful of gospel groups, such as Smith's Sacred Singers, recorded extensively and sold hundreds of thousands of copies.) From 1925 to 1935, about 25 percent of the various country or old-time series released consisted of gospel music, or what was then called "old time sacred singing." But during the 1930s, as the growth and merger of record companies made regional programming impractical, gospel quartets appeared less and less on major labels. Thus, by the end of the war, gospel singers were relieved to note the formation of dozens of new record companies, many of them small and flexible and able to respond again to a regional audience. In 1940, three companies (Victor, Decca, ARC) dominated the record business; by 1949 the annual *Billboard* report listed some 400 record companies. Several of these companies, such as Bibletone, Sacred, White Church, specialized exclusively in gospel music, while many of the regional labels like Bama (Birmingham), President (Little Rock), Rich-R-Tone (Johnson City, Tennessee), and Blue Ridge (North Carolina) were receptive to local quartets who had regional appeal. Since these regional companies have been virtually ignored by students of American music and culture, we have little idea of their histories, the men who ran them, or even the scope of their activity. The larger companies, though, like Bibletone and Rich-R-Tone, had releases numbering into the hundreds, and were soon advertising in *Billboard* and other trade publications right next to the major labels.

Many independent record companies offered custom services, where artists could have their own recordings released on their own personal label. This soon became a favorite device for the new gospel quartets, who found they could sell records through the mail and at personal appearances, and who liked the complete artistic control they enjoyed on custom labels. Exactly which group was the first to have its own custom label is a question which has not yet been resolved. The Blackwood Brothers, working from their base in Shenendoah, Iowa, began recording their own records in the studios of KMA by late 1946 or early 1947, releasing them on the "Blackwood Brothers" label, graced with a logo that included a photo of the group. Other quartets like the Rangers and the Statesmen soon followed suit, and for a time one group headed by Wally Fowler (cf. below) had a "Record of the Month" club.

Gospel song publishing was changing as well. For years, country singers had been able to augment their income by selling song folios of their favorite radio songs, with pictures of themselves or their bands. Gospel publishing, though, had naturally remained in the hands of the publishing companies, and pretty much confined to the regular "singing convention" books which seldom made mention of any performers. Stamps-Baxter was offering a service whereby any customer who would take 1,000 copies of a particular songbook would be offered an option whereby "we print your name on the covers and leave ours off entirely," creating instant songbooks for singers or evangelists: instant, but hardly representative of the singers' real repertoire. Now, as quartets became more independent, they began to design and sell their own songbooks, giving photos, a history of the group, and favorite songs. At first, these were small, locally printed books, but by 1954 the big quartets like the Blackwoods and the Statesmen had graduated to slick handsome folios in the manner of leading country and pop stars of the day. Lee Roy Abernathy took matters even further in the late 1940s when he began to publish some of his most popular songs in sheet music form. Veteran gospel singers and writers—including members of Abernathy's own quartet—were taken aback by the idea: why should a fan pay fifty cents for one song when he could buy an entire Stamps-Baxter convention songbook for thirty-five cents? But Abernathy's songs were popular enough—and promoted well enough—that people did buy. The new singers and songwriters were also learning about copyrights and royalties: gone were the days when a songwriter would trade the rights to his song to a Stamps-Baxter company for 25 copies of the songbook it was to be published in.

While the most drastic changes of the late 1940s dealt with how gospel music was presented and promoted, equally important changes were occurring in singing styles and song-writing styles. Young writers began to look to other sources of inspiration besides the singing convention stalwarts like Albert Brumley, Eugene Wright, J. R. Baxter, Jr., and others. Writers like Vep Ellis, Mosie Lister, Lee Roy Abernathy, and Wally Fowler began to incorporate into their songs echoes of pop music, blues, black gospel, and even jazz. Most of this new crop of writers came from the South, and had deep roots in traditional gospel as well as folk music; they also, though, were very much aware of the newest country and pop sounds. One of Wally Fowler's first gospel hits, "Pray, Pray, Pray for the U.S.A.," merged World War II patriotism with a God-is-on-our-side theme. The smooth harmony cowboy singing style of the Sons of the Pioneers emerged in Abernathy's "Riding the Range for Jesus." The fondness for metaphor so common in country music merged with the topical trend and the gospel to produce startling pieces like "Jesus Hits Like an Atom

Bomb." But the song which typified so much of the new style and theme, and the one which was the most successful of all of them, was a piece called "Gospel Boogie."

In fact, "Gospel Boogie" and the story behind it can serve as a microcosm for many of the changes that were happening to white gospel music during this time. The song was popularized by a group called the Homeland Harmony Quartet, an Atlanta-based foursome that had been founded in 1942. Original members included Connor Hall, brothers Otis and James McCoy, B. C. Robinson, and pianist Hovie Lister. Hall came from a background in singing schools and church music at Greensboro, North Carolina; the McCoys, natives of north Alabama, were for years associated with the Tennessee Music and Printing Company, one of the leading convention songbook publishers. Lister, a generation younger than Hall, had also been born in Greenville, and worked his way through the Stamps-Baxter school of music; later he was to become famous as the leader of the Statesmen. All members of the quartet, thus, were solidly grounded in the singing school-publisher tradition, and nothing dramatic might have happened to them had they not met up, in 1945, with Lee Roy Abernathy. Abernathy that year replaced Lister on piano, and began to push the group into commercialization and even controversy. Born in Georgia in 1913, Abernathy and his family used quartet singing as an escape from the rigors of working in a textile mill, and he was already singing with his father's ATCO Quartet when they recorded an acapella version of "The Rich Young Ruler" for Columbia in 1927. In the late 1930s Abernathy was trying to sell piano lessons by mail, and soon thereafter he did a stint with the highly professional group, the Rangers. For a time he even headed a country band called the Modern Mountaineers. The latter experiences marked him from the other members of the Homeland Harmony group, and made him less nervous about overtly promoting and commercializing his music. As early as 1947, Abernathy, who had become the quartet's manager, embroiled them in controversy when he wrote and had them record a song about the tragic fire in the Winecoff Hotel in Atlanta, still remembered as America's worst hotel fire. For weeks the letter columns of the Atlanta newspapers were full of letters either condemning the song for poor taste, or celebrating it for the sympathy and insight. Not until years later did other members of the Homeland Harmony Quartet learn that Abernathy himself had written some of the letters under assumed names to generate attention for the song.

No such efforts were really necessary for "Gospel Boogie"; it generated its own controversy a year later when the quartet started doing it on radio and at concerts. While the term "boogie" had been used by black piano players since the 1920s, the style had been popularized in the early 1940s by the success of Tommy Dorsey's arrangement of Pinetop Smith's "Boogie Woogie," and by dozens of pop follow-ups like the Andrews Sisters's "Boogie Woogie Bugle Boy." Though pop definitions of "boogie" came to include almost any uptempo style, the original concept was based on a 8-to-the-bar number built around the bass runs of the piano. For some years, gospel piano players had been incorporating elements of ragtime and stride piano into their back-up and solo styles, and it was not surprising that writers like Abernathy and Mosie Lister (no relation to Hovie) would use boogie elements as well. The problem with "Gospel Boogie" was that the boogie influence was very prominent, in the title and in the fact that the quartet actually sang the piano bass run as part of their arrangement.

Though "Gospel Boogie" was copyrighted in November 1947, the Homeland Harmony Quartet did not record it for White Church until early 1948. Their original version attracted immediate attention, and began to sell very well for a gospel song on a small label. Some of the advertising was later to insist that over two million copies of the record were sold, but Connor Hall places the true sales figure of their version at more like 200,000. (Such exaggeration of sales in trade publication ads helped spur sales, and was quite typical in the late 1940s.) Within a few months, "Gospel Boogie" was also recorded by at least ten other artists, including Sister Rosetta Tharpe, Red Foley, Wally Fowler, a black quartet called the Pilgrim Travellers, and others.

Even after the popularity of this version of the song died down, Wally Fowler continued to promote the song, and a few years later took it to Randy Wood, then president of Dot Records. Wood got the song to Pat Boone, then at the height of his popularity, and he recorded another hit version of it (using the title "A Wonderful Time Up There") which in 1958 reached Number Ten of the *Billboard* charts. Today the song is reasonably well established as a standard with many gospel artists, white and black.

"Gospel Boogie" served as a harbinger of a debate within the gospel community itself, as the ideas and values of the older musicians ran head-on into the ideas and values of the new professionals. Popular though it was, Connor Hall recalls, there were many occasions when the leaders of a church or singing convention where the Homeland Harmony Quartet was appearing would specifically request that the group *not* perform "Gospel Boogie." Letters to the Atlanta papers attacked the song on moral grounds; author Lee Roy Abernathy defended it in other letters; noting that "boogie" was just another synonym for rhythm, a cornerstone for all music, Abernathy went on to say: "When I wrote 'Gospel Boogie' I was inspired to write it. I felt it was one means of reaching the distant places where no ministers go . . . no singers sing, in juke jives, etc." Abernathy, though, seemed unable eventually to overcome the connotations of "boogie" and the song's later success was attained under its alternate title, "A Wonderful Time Up There."

The real debate was yet to come though, and centered on issues much larger than a single song. For some years the singing convention publishers had been fond of having large, all-night group singings to mark the end of a term, or year; in

1940 Stamps-Baxter held one that almost filled the Cotton Bowl. The professional quartets soon found they could adapt this tradition to their own ends; starting about 1945, the Homeland Harmony Quartet and the Rangers, then on opposing radio stations in Atlanta, staged a "Battle of Song" in Atlanta's Municipal Auditorium; for weeks prior to the concert, the two quartets—who were good friends—built up tension by asserting that Jim Waits, the bass singer for the Homeland Harmony Quartet, would run Rangers bass singer Arnold Hyles out of town. The "Battle" drew a capacity crowd at the auditorium, and after it was all over, and the bills paid, the quartet members—all ten of them—found to their amazement that they had cleared over a thousand dollars a man. Hall recalls: "That was the first time I had ever heard of a quartet in a concert in one night making that much money."

"The Battle of Song" became a regular feature in Atlanta, and within a couple of years was used as a model for a much more elaborate promotional device that was to become synonymous with gospel music in the 1950s: the "all-night singing." And with this innovation, a man entered the gospel scene who was to become one of its most colorful—and controversial—figures: Wally Fowler.

Fowler came from a background of singing conventions and quartets and rural poverty. Born the youngest child of a sharecropper near Adairsville, Georgia, in 1917, he had begun singing with professional groups by the time he was eighteen. In 1936 he started singing baritone for the John Daniel Quartet, one of the most popular and successful groups to come out of Alabama; working with Daniel, he was exposed to the grueling round of one-night stands and local singing conventions sandwiched between radio programs. But in 1940 the Daniel Quartet landed a job on WSM's Grand Ole Opry, and the group began to diversify their music; a poster of the time advertises that the quartet features "Folk, Sacred, and Old-Time Ballads" as well as "Pop Songs, Novelties, and Variety Entertainment." As their repertoire expanded, so did their audience, so that by 1944 the Daniel Quartet was one of the nation's most popular country acts; Fowler began to write songs, many of them nongospel sorts like "Propaganda Papa" and "Mother's Prayer."

In 1944 he decided to form his own group and try to make it as full-time country singer—a trend that was to be repeated in years to come by artists as different as Martha Carson and the Oak Ridge Boys. With a string band called the Georgia Clodhoppers, Fowler moved to Knoxville, where he was very active in booking, promotion, publishing, and songwriting. One of his songs, "That's How Much I Love You," was to be recorded widely by singers like Eddy Arnold, Bing Crosby, and Frank Sinatra. During his tenure at Knoxville, he got in the habit of giving regular free performances to school children in the nearby town of Oak Ridge, many of whose parents worked at the highly secret atomic research facility there. The concerts were so successful that he began to call his group the Oak Ridge Quartet, and began to think more and more about going back into gospel full time. The opportunity came in 1945 when WSM rehired him and the Oak Ridge Quartet, first for a series of early morning (5:30 A.M.) daily programs, then later as a regular on the portion of the Opry that was broadcast over the NBC network. This gave the group exposure across the country from 1945 to 1950.

Calling on his own experience as a country singer and publisher, and on his earlier stint with John Daniel, Fowler began to apply some of his successful promotion techniques to gospel music. Soon after he returned to Nashville, he founded Wallace Fowler Publications in December 1945; next to Acuff-Rose, it was one of the earliest country publishing houses in Nashville, and for a couple of years was very active in releasing song folios of popular country radio artists. These folios usually contained no more than 20 songs, but added photos and biographies of the stars; Fowler issued folios by Johnnie and Jack, Eddy Arnold, Milton Estes, Cliff Carlisle, in addition to his own Oak Ridge Quartet, and negotiated distribution rights for at least one collection of Albert E. Brumley songs. While the publications certainly had a gospel flavor, by and large they were aimed at the country market; Fowler also, in 1946, began to work as a talent scout and representative for New York publisher Edwin H. Morris. Turning away from his affiliation with Capitol Records, Fowler also started his own record label, selling the product through his "Record-of-the-Month Club." Through such channels were later Oak Ridge Quartet hits like "Pray, Pray, Pray for the U.S.A." distributed.

His greatest success, however, was promotion. In 1948 he fused two earlier traditions in gospel music: the "all-night singing" that had been for years a feature at the end of the term of Stamps-Baxter singing schools, and the "battle of the quartets" idea initiated by Abernathy in Atlanta in 1946. He borrowed the scope of the all-night singing, and expanded on the idea of using professional quartets as the entertainment. Instead of just two quartets battling it out, though, Fowler decided to book six, seven, or even a dozen. He first tried out his idea on Friday, November 5, 1948, when he booked "25 Quartets" and "100 Singers on Stage" into the Ryman auditorium in downtown Nashville; the program was scheduled to run from 8:30 P.M. to 4:00 A.M., and the admission was seventy-five cents for the duration. For an hour, between 11:00 and 12:00 P.M., the procedings were to be broadcast over WSM. A story in the following morning's Nashville *Tennessean* offered a detailed account of the novel event:

SPIRITUALS SWING THROUGH LONG NIGHT
Nashville's midnight gaiety faded away.
And then the early morning air was split with an alien tune—the rising sound of singing voices, recalling visions of a lowly manger, a bright star and three bearded men.
At 1 a.m. a street cleaner lent a questioning ear; at 2 a policeman slowly paced his beat to "Crossing Over Jordan." Later an unsteady sojourner turned his eyes heavenward at "When the Fire Comes Down." And then the milk man perked up at "Dese Bones a Gwinna Rise Agin."
And it was 4 a.m. before the audience and Nashville's first "All-

Night Singing," held last night in Ryman auditorium, dispersed into the rainy night.

Several States Participate

Some 150 entertainers from several states took part in the jammed auditorium. The program began at 8 p.m.

Singers—men, women and children—from Tennessee, Georgia, Alabama, Iowa, Texas, West Virginia, Kentucky and other states were on hand to dispense Gospel tunes, old and new, to an enthusiastic, shuttling audience, a great many of whom held their seats until the passing of the final strains.

It was something new in the entertainment field in Middle Tennessee, and its sponsor, Wally Fowler, said he hopes to make it a periodical event.

Such well-known combinations as Milton Estes and Musical Millers quartet, Fowler's Oak Ridge quartet, the Speer Family and the Blackwood brothers delighted the audience with their various renditions of popular hymns.

Crowds From Afar

Practically every seat in the auditorium was taken at the beginning of the all-night program at 8:30 o'clock. Later, some of the visitors from more remote areas began shuffling out in tiny knots. Sleepy-eyed youngsters, sliding fast into the sandman's arms, fell over into the vacated seats.

All night long the booming voices of the singers poured over the resounding walls of the cornerless old auditorium.

Frequently an over-enthusiastic listener supplemented the fading echoes with a belated chord of a well-loved tune.

By 4 a.m. eyes were flickering heavily, but for those who remained until the last it was the first experience of an interesting occasion which many of them no doubt would duplicate.

This first "sing" attracted some 1800 patrons; in addition to the slick, popular quartets, the show featured important links with the older singing convention publishers: Frank Stamps, then president of his own Stamps Quartet Publishing Company, appeared with his quartet, and James D. Walbert, the grandson of pioneer publisher James D. Vaughan, displayed his considerable abilities as a piano soloist. It was successful enough that Fowler began to stage regular monthly singings in the Ryman auditorium, hiring the quartets for a flat fee and doing all the publicity himself; for the quartets, the show meant publicity and the chance to be heard nationwide over the WSM radio hook-up. After the second singing, on December 31, 1948, mail about the program began to pour in, and publicity photos show the Oak Ridge Quartet standing behind huge piles of letters. In his second anniversary program, for November 3, 1950, Fowler wrote: "Month by month more and more people from all over the country are coming to the Ryman Auditorium to see and hear the most outstanding quartets in the nation." Fowler was also taking the Oak Ridge Quartet on tour between monthly shows, and many of these road shows also took the form of all-night singings. By 1955 his formula was so successful that it was the subject of an article in *Collier's Magazine*, where his "road show" was described as playing "to audiences of up to 15,000 a week in some 200 towns and cities in 38 states each season"; certain shows in Alabama or North Carolina drew up to 10,000 people for a single night. By the time Fowler printed up the program for his tenth anniversary singing in 1958, he was able to claim that he "had promoted and conducted a total of one thousand and nine All Nite Singings in the South and Southeast," and had travelled "an average of one hundred thousand miles per year."

Fowler was a master showman who ran his all-night sings like an emcee from one of the new fast-moving television variety shows. He admitted that his show format was a time-honored one: "Make 'em laugh, make 'em cry, make 'em laugh again. That way you entertain 'em as well as make 'em feel a spiritual blessing." On a typical show, each group would come out and do a 20-25 minute set, often returning once or even twice in the course of a night. Fowler hovered about each group, talking to them, joking with them, occasionally joining in with them. Groups ranged from the big quartets like the Blackwoods, the Statesmen, the Homeland Harmony, to the older groups like the Chuck Wagon Gang and the Rangers, to the family groups like the Goodman Family and the Speer Family, to child prodigies like the Johnson Sisters. Local groups that had won singing contests were often added to the program, and Fowler would announce from the stage the various churches or civic organizations that had been attending the singing as a group. Local ministers often were asked to deliver the opening prayer. Nor did Fowler shy away from attention-getting stunts, such as letting the Statesmen run up and down the aisles as they sang "When the Saints Go Marching In," or calling twenty-three ministers of all denominations on stage and having them sing "Amazing Grace." There was little "congregational" singing as such—usually an opening and closing song and perhaps a round of "Turn Your Radio On" to open the portion of the "sing" that was broadcast.

The shift away from the older singing convention format was almost complete. Whereas the audience at the singing conventions participated in a major way in the singing, the Fowler audiences were passive, listening audiences. Most of the performers at a singing convention were gifted amateurs, singing for their own enjoyment or inspiration; most of the performers at the all-night sings were the new professionals, slick, smooth, clever, costumed, wise-cracking, and singing to make money. The singers at a singing convention were trained musicians, able to sight-read shape notes with ease; many of the new professionals sang by ear, and had difficulty reading from the songbooks. Connor Hall recalls that many of the new slick quartets got to hate being invited to the singing conventions, because although they would be the center of attention when they performed in concert on Saturday night, they would often have to suffer the embarrassment of sitting with their mouths closed on Sunday as the convention went about its sight-reading singing. For years the singing conventions invited quartets to provide special music and attract crowds; now the newer quartets were more and more anxious to break off from this association.

This finally boiled over into print in 1949 and 1950. Rupert Cravens, writing in the editorial pages of *Vaughan's Family Visitor*, then one of the main organs for the singing convention publishers, launched a sustained attack against the "gospel jamborees" in late 1949 and 1950. In one issue he wrote:

> Why should people who love the Lord and clean Christian society have to listen to the music of the "juke box" to find a medium of expression toward God? Would Wesley or Toplady have written poems to be set to some of the modern boogy-woogy songs that so many of the so-called better quartets go wild about? Why should men who are supposed to love the Lord make for their most popular phonograph records and "song hits" a type of songs that is too cheap in the light of God's holy purpose to deserve mention? Why should a so-called Christian audience go crazy over an all-night jamboree which often opened with a prayer but is thereafter carried on as if there were no God? What are we to say about Sunday conventions that often have for their special attraction quartets and groups whose breath smells strongly of the beer joint?

The conventional publishers were also correct in their perception that the growing popularity of all-night singing jamborees, and the rise of professional quartets, posed a serious threat to their well-being. The companies' entire economic structure was founded on the singing convention; there was little way it could ever adapt to the newer system. But some of the objections by people like Cravens were doubtless also founded on genuine moral concerns. Values were shifting, and a music that was once an expression of religious belief was now a business. It is no wonder that by mid-1950 Cravens was comparing the singing jamborees to the threat of Communism.

The quartets, for their part, saw the singing convention publishers and their supporters as standing in the way of their artistic and commercial development. In 1948 Lee Roy Abernathy published a fascinating book designed to serve as a handbook for the new professional quartets; in it he enunciated a ringing attack on the opponents of professional gospel. "Should gospel quartets charge? They most certainly should, and they really ought to charge more than they do. They have spent a lifetime learning to sing for you. . . Does your minister preach for nothing? . . .does anyone do anything for nothing? . . .Does the painter paint for nothing? . . .does anyone do anything for nothing? . . .No! Neither should the Gospel Quartet man. If you are one of those tight-fisted cheap, chronic gripers that wouldn't give a dime to see ANYTHING . . . you shouldn't be allowed to go to church, or to have singers in your community. The general public has in recent years become educated to the fact that GOSPEL QUARTETS ARE THE REASON FOR THEIR SINGING BEING THE BEST IT HAS EVER BEEN. Only a few ignorant, jealous-hearted back biters are keeping Gospel music back. However, it is going forward now at the most terrific rate it has in years."

Abernathy, in the end, was right, and the commercial quartet format did win out. He and Fowler were by no means alone responsible for the change; the remarkable story of the Blackwood Brothers (only touched on here) and their adaptation of black gospel styles and songs into white settings was vitally important, as were numerous other acts and individuals. But for all intents and purposes, the battle had been won by 1955. By then there were a dozen musical gospel road shows like Fowler's touring the South, and promotion and booking techniques were becoming as sophisticated as those in other forms of pop music. The 1953 *Billboard* "Country and Western Artists' Directory" listed 23 full-time professional gospel groups among its 200-odd acts; virtually all of them had regular radio affiliations, primarily in the South, and most had regular recording contracts. Fifteen of them were booked not by Fowler but by the McCormick Gospel Booking Agency, located at the Cherokee Hotel in Tallahassee, Florida. Some of the big names, like the Blackwood Brothers, Frank Stamps, and Stuart Hamblen, still did their own booking, and a couple (Martha Carson, the Jordanaires) were being handled by the newly emerging Nashville agencies. Most of the quartets handled by McCormick did only eight to twelve personal appearances per month, suggesting they still toured only on weekends. This was in contrast to the Blackwoods (25 personals per month), Frank Stamps (20 personals per month),

Martha Carson (25 personals per month), or George Beverly Shea (20 personals per month). One by one the old song convention publishing giants— Vaughan, Henson, Winsett—were bought out by the new publishing companies organized by quartets like the Blackwoods, the Statesmen, and the Oak Ridge Boys. In some cases, the new owners simply stopped publishing convention books, hoping to eradicate completely the singing convention movement and turn all the gospel convention singers into listeners at concerts. Many of the singing conventions have disbanded, and the songbook publishers, which at one time in the 1930s numbered over fifty companies, have shrunk to a handful of four or five. It was part of the tragic price white gospel music paid for entrance into the arena of mainstream pop music, and atrophy of the singing conventions represented the loss of another vital link to gospel music's rich folk tradition.

A Note on Sources

Much of the material in the above essay was drawn from personal interviews with the following: James Walbert (Birmingham, June 1978); Mrs. W. B. Walbert (James D. Vaughan's daughter) (Lawrenceburg, Tennessee, July 1978); Otis McCoy (Jasper, Alabama, June 1978); Connor Hall (Cleveland, Tennessee, February 1980).

Rupert Craven's quote was taken from *Vaughan's Family Visitor*, April 1950, page 2; a detailed account of Wally Fowler's all-night gospel singing in 1948 can be found in the Nashville *Tennessean*, November 6, 1948, page 1; Lee Roy Abernathy's statements about professional quartets come from his *It* (Atlanta: Abernathy Printing Company, 1948). Accounts of the success of "Gospel Boogie" can be read in *Billboard*, April 10, 1948; an interesting account of the Homeland Harmony Quartet can be found in *Radio Mirror*, January 10, 1948. I have also drawn on an unpublished manuscript by Connor Hall, "The Origin of the Gospel Quartet."

General accounts of the history of white gospel music include Lois Blackwell, *The Wings of the Dove* (Norfolk, Virginia: Donning Company, 1978); Jesse Burt and Duane Allen, *A History of Gospel Music* (Nashville: K & S Press, 1971); and David Crawford, "Gospel Songs in Court: From Rural Music to Urban Industry in the 1950s," *Journal of Popular Culture*, 11 (1977), 551-568. Also very useful is Stanley Brobston's unpublished dissertation,"A Brief History of White Southern Gospel Music" (New York University, 1977).

I have also learned much from informal discussions with Harlan Daniel, Stanley Brobston, Doyne Horsley, and Jack Calaway, and to them I owe an important debt.

The Secularization of Black Gospel Music

Anthony Heilbut

IN THE EIGHTEENTH CENTURY, John Wesley wondered in straightforward Methodist style, why the devil should have all the good tunes, as if saints and sinners could divide music up into spiritual and secular provinces. Perhaps in other times and places, sacred and worldly music comprised discrete entities. But the music of the black folk church has been grappling with secular forces since the early twenties, a period coinciding with the massive distribution of recordings for black audiences, if not earlier. There has been a continual dialectic between the "songs of Zion" and the "devil's tunes," and as happens in the most interesting dialectical encounters, this particular conflict ushered in a subtle intermingling of extremes, and a consequent confusion of forms and habits. As a happy result, the twenty-year period from 1940 to 1960, Gospel's Golden Age, produced an outpouring of creative talent surpassed only by jazz. Twenty years later, through other dialectical twists, black gospel finds itself besieged by the worldly appeals it warded off so well so long. The enemy this time is not the devil—as Thomas Mann reminded us, Lucifer makes a splendid music critic—but the forces of the marketplace. The secularization of black gospel music has evolved from a generalized commercialization, not merely of gospel. And this development has social and political implications that quite dwarf the problem of whether the music is as good as it once was.

It is a commonplace that modern gospel music dates from the early thirties. But there are certain constants in black church music that go back much longer. I would stress the Dr. Watts hymns—named after the English hymnodist, Isaac Watts—both for the beauty of their solemn cadences, and for their characteristic performing styles—the blue-noted keening and humming, known as "moaning," and the intricately convoluted melismatic patterns, compact of slurs, spoken interpolations, and absolute rhythmic freedom. These seem to me the essential characteristics of the black gospel style. Dr. Watts's singing allows for liberties, for elaborate ornamentation, always, however, signaled by "spirit feel," an elusive mood that can make a hymn like "Amazing Grace" or "The Day Is Past and Gone" go on for anywhere from five minutes to half an hour, if the spirit is right and the singers so inclined.

Obviously not all black church songs were as poignant as these evocations of hard times and imminent death. The happier, rhythmic songs were accompanied by the holy dance, the "shout." (Incidentally, the word "shouting" is also used to describe the holy dancing of white Pentecostals.) Shout steps vary with the individual. Once they may have been standardized, just as once the only accompaniment was hand-clapping and foot-tapping. Today when someone gets happy, he or she may dance to a full instrumental ensemble, and the steps may be extremely flamboyant and acrobatic. What is constant, again, is the emphasis on spirit feel, and the oft-expressed conviction of one's shout steps originates with his or her conversion, and so is as individual a public display as his or her way of walking or talking. The very term "holy dance" calls attention to itself. Anyone who has seen holy dancing in white Pentecostal churches, much less the meetings of the *soi-disant* charismatics, will understand how distinctive holy dancing in black churches is, and how influential: a perception evident in the works of Alvin Ailey or the dances performed on "Soul Train."

The social functions of the black preacher have been well analyzed. I would like to point out the premium congregations place on his *showmanship*. As the ethos dictates that he must be "called" and "sent," so the dictates of the spirit will color his preaching, causing him to growl, moan, chant, and even sing his words, to move about freely, to run, to crawl, to shout, in a word, to "clown." Clowning, as the description of showmanship, is an ambivalent term among gospel singers. Everyone knows it's wrong to put on, yet every singer or preacher knows it is necessary and well-nigh universal. As a larger phenomenon, clowning as it manifests itself in gospel, blues, soul, or for that matter, country and western and white gospel, is worth some real attention. Once again, it evokes a dialectical response: the congregation or audience may applaud the performer's generosity while feeling a certain superiority over any person who must work so hard merely to earn an Amen or a hand-clap.

Preachers were the best-selling religious artists of the 1920s. Their sermons were frequently on religious topics, punctuated by ecstatic outbursts from a few members of the congregation imported for the recording session—one wonders how these saints must have felt, waiting in those old Okeh and Columbia studios while the blues singers and vaudevillians took their turn to record. Another theme, still common, was children's mistreatment of their mothers. There were frequent song services, especially in recordings of Holiness preachers. But what's interesting in terms of the secularization of church music is the inordinate number of sermons on secular topics, or inspired by secular, i.e., blues tunes. For example, the Reverend J. M. Gates could ignore the witty double entendres of Thomas A. Dorsey's "It's Tight Like That" and use the expression to describe conditions during the Depression: "Times are tight but it's going to be tighter than that." One of his best-selling records, "Dead Cat on the Line," derived from a folk-saying common to black and white Southerners, "If a child don't favor his father some way, there's a dead cat on the line." Gates's record is at once a self-righteous castigation of adultery and illegitimacy, a subversive comment on the usual canonization of mother, and something bordering on risque comedy. Church audiences still appreciate comparable displays of wit. Such popular preachers as the Reverend C. L. Franklin, the Reverend W. Leo Daniels, or the Reverend Johnny L. Jones will take the titles of currently popular tunes—e.g., "Who's Making Love to Your Old Lady While You're Out Making Love"—and convert them into spiritual sentiments. Audiences applaud the bravado involved, in these hair-breadth escapes from the devil's clutches.

On a less obvious level, there is a worldly cast to many gospel sermons simply because American evangelism is thoroughly infused with materialistic and pragmatic perspectives. In good empirical tradition, American evangelicals expect their signs and wonders to be visible, manifested by cures from illnesses and relief from financial burdens. This abandonment of the transcendent for the transparent can make for the expressive art of a Dorothy Love Coates singing "When I was down and out, you know I didn't have a dime," or for the startling display of a middle-class white charismatic, confessing on the TV "700 Club" that her husband is unfaithful and being subsequently slain in the spirit as a Catholic priest anoints her with oil. But the underlying theme—God helps his saints in this world—already focuses on the secular as the realm of significant action.

During the twenties, along with preachers, the most successful religious recordings were made by quartets. The quartet style is much older than the gospel group style, ushered in during the thirties under the influence of leaders like Roberta Martin. In fact, quartet was once ubiquitous, not merely the preferred but virtually the only recorded group singing. So, on the recordings of the Reverend Gates, when Clara Hudman, later known as the Georgia Peach, begins to lead a hymn, the congregants, male and female, immediately take up easy four part harmony. Likewise, if you listen to the many religious recordings included in the Library of Congress archives, you will find quartet sung by men, women, and children, in factories, log camps, prisons, and plantations. The pleasures of quartet singing are both personal—the joys of holding one's part— and communal—the construction of intricate chords and harmonies.

Quartet has always been largely a male province, an institution of working class black life akin in its traditional claims to athletic teams or fraternal lodges. It has also undergone the most changes. A 1920s preacher may resemble a 1970s preacher; the Holiness congregations of the late twenties are echoed by the small church services occasionally heard on late-night radio. But no quartets today sound like the 1920s quartets; one obvious difference is the introduction of instruments, dating from the early fifties. Quartets have always been susceptible to worldly influences; perhaps because their image has seldom been as "consecrated" as that of the female gospel singers. The two leading quartets of the twenties, the Norfolk Jubilee Singers and the Birmingham Jubilee Singers, recorded both religious and worldly tunes; the Norfolks calling themselves the Norfolk Jazz Quartet for tunes like "Jelly Roll Blues" or "Strut Miss Lizzie." On the other hand, there could be no confusion about the sanctified singers affiliated with the Church of God in Christ and other Holiness denominations. Their recordings were more raucous and syncopated than the more sedate Baptist and Methodist quartets, and their lead singers already more stylized and flamboyant. But the individuality, for those who understood, was simply a sign of spiritual inspiration. Women like Arizona Dranes, Jessie May Hill, Mother McCollum, Bessie Johnson, and Clara Hudman looked forward to the great gospel divas of later years. The sanctified pianists and guitarists—for many years, instruments were forbidden in Baptist and Methodist churches as the devil's tools—exhibited a virtuoso technique that would later influence jazz and rhythm and blues. And Blind Willie Johnson, the best male religious singer of the twenties, sings in a manner that still seems contemporary;

his duets with his wife are echoed today in the work of Brother and Sister Pugh, the Consolers, and Blind Willie himself performs with the showmanly zeal and growling authority of the very best modern "hard" or "preaching" quartet leads.

The religious songs recorded in the twenties included traditional spirituals, topical songs like "The Florida Storm" ("short skirts and filthy dances have caused our hearts to bleed, And now our country's filled up with every wicked deed"), Church of God in Christ shout songs, and two forerunners of modern gospel tunes, white evangelical songs and the compositions of C. A. Tindley. Every decade of this century, some white religious songs have swept black congregations—from tunes in the teens and twenties like "Hold to God's Unchanging Hand," "Life Is Like a Mountain Railroad," "When I Take My Vacation in Heaven," to the thirties— "Precious Memories," "Will the Circle Be Unbroken," "I'll Fly Away," "Never Grow Old"—to the currently popular "He Touched Me" and "Rise Again." Conversely, C. A. Tidley's songs became standards in white churches as well as black. A Philadelphia Methodist minister, Tindley composed in the 1890s and early 1900s, a series of hymns—"Stand By Me," "Take Your Burdens to the Lord," "We'll Understand It Better By and By," "Let Jesus Fix It for You," "The Storm is Passing Over," "I'll Overcome," the origin of "We Shall Overcome"—that managed to combine folk sayings and melodies with the standard diction and harmonies of white hymns. Tindley was the inspiration of Thomas A. Dorsey, the most famous gospel composer. His importance can be gauged by the number of Tindley singing societies extant by 1930. The songs of another gospel writer, Lucie E. Campbell, were also recorded as early as 1927.

Yet it was only with the 1930s that gospel music came into prominence. This was largely due to the promotional efforts of Thomas A. Dorsey, a former blues singer and composer, who brought into the church a jazz bounce that tempered the more special yet also more strident sanctified rhythms. By 1931, the Famous Blue Jay Singers of Birmingham, Alabama, had recorded a Dorsey tune; by 1934, a Dorsey tune showed up on a Library of Congress recording made on a Louisiana plantation; by 1938, Sister Rosetta Tharpe had taken his "Hide Me in Thy Bosom," neutered its religious sentiments, in a version called "Rock Me" that became a national "race records" hit; and, perhaps, most auspicious of all, by 1939, four of Dorsey's compositions were included in a songbook, printed in shape-notes, that was widely distributed in white evangelical congregations. Dorsey was obviously a child of the blues. So too, in his own way, was the Reverend W. Herbert Brewster, a Memphis Baptist minister—to my mind, the finest of all modern gospel composers—who had been friendly with W. C. Handy. Brewster's early tunes emphasized 16-bar blues that began in the traditional, slow-paced manner of Dr. Watts hymns, and invariably, in an ecumenical gesture, shifted from verses sung to no beat to choruses that rocked in sanctified fashion: Brewster's tunes, especially as arranged in the 1940s and 1950s by Clara Ward, Marion Williams, and Mahalia Jackson, grew even more rhythmically adventurous. He cultivated waltz rhythms and multiple changes in tempo, the beat accelerating even as the lyrics turned simpler: e. g., "Weeping May Endure for a Night" that begins with a lyric as prolix as an eighteenth-century hymn, and culminates in the repeated shout, "He'll make it all right, all right, all right."

Gospel became a recognized form in the thirties, with its capital, Chicago, the home of Dorsey. Outside of the Church of God in Christ singers, the important pioneer soloists tended to be Midwesterners: Sallie Martin and Roberta Martin, both leaders of influential groups; Willie Mae Ford Smith, who Thomas A. Dorsey believes could have been Bessie Smith's superior; and Mahalia Jackson who drew on the approaches of two Smiths, Bessie and Willie Mae Ford. The gospel sound galvanized quartet as well. While the Norfolk Jubilee Singers continued to perform highly sophisticated arrangements of spiritual and secular tunes, the most important thirties quartet, the Golden Gate Jubilee Quartet, derived some of their more exhilarating tempos from the Holiness churches of their native Virginia. The quartet recorded Dr. Watts hymns and Dorsey compositions; and emphasized showmanly leads, at least two of whom, Bill Landford and Henry Owens, were in a newer gospel groove. The Gates, from their debut, also included secular tunes; their recording of "Stormy Weather" with its intense, slurred harmonies sounds uncannily like the gospel-influenced doo-wop ballads of the 1950s. Similarly, the former gospel singer Lil Green in her "Romance in the Dark" (1940) or Rosetta Tharpe in her "I'm a Short Fat Mama" (1941) applied highly stylized gospel devices: word repetitions, slurred lines, virtuoso vocal effects, such as sustained notes and interval leaps. Meanwhile the most influential gospel quartet of all, the Soul Stirrers, had moved from their native Texas to Chicago. The group's founder, Silas Roy Crain, had decided to reject the more rugged, vocally demanding approach of the earlier quartets—"we simply couldn't do that stuff"—for a sweet, crooning background and a brand new emphasis on the lead singer. Their most influential lead, R. H. Harris, had a twang and yodel reminiscent of both blues and white country singers. Harris would sing what he calls delayed time, riding behind and ahead of his background: syncopations already familiar in sanctified and female gospel, but new for quartet.

By the 1940s, gospel music began to surface in secular music settings, e. g., New York's Cafe Society Downtown, where Rosetta Tharpe, the Dixie Hummingbirds, and the Golden Gates appeared. Even before the postwar boom in recordings, gospel groups began to pack large churches, halls, and stadiums. Art Rupp, founder of Specialty Records, says by the mid-forties he began to notice his leading blues singers sneaking around to gospel concerts for inspiration. The preeminent female blues singer of this era was Dinah Washington, quondam lead of the Sallie Martin Singers.

Washington was the first major black popular star to be totally unembarrassed in her exploitation of her gospel roots. Characteristically, with the years, she would color her phrasing with ironic innuendos, as if every other phrase was in double quotes. Actually the shift from choir soloist to Evil Gal or from bawdy to sublime has its gospel analogues, as can be witnessed by anyone who has observed the sensual flirtations with their audiences of women singers like Mahalia Jackson, Marion Williams, or Inez Andrews. Incidentally, up to the arrival of Ray Charles, Dinah Washington is the only nongospel singer I saw in the 1950s, who could command an Apollo Theater audience with the know-how of a gospel trouper.

The forties also expanded gospel's range to include specifically political issues, in part due to the war, in part to the early stirrings of freedom movements. So the Golden Gates recorded attacks on segregation as well as "Stalin Wasn't Stalling," a kind of Popular Front anthem; the disc jockey, Otis Jackson, composed a paean to President Roosevelt— "Tell me why you like Roosevelt, he was no kin . . . he gave me a job and a comfortable home"—as well as "Sure Do Need Him Now," a listing of prominent black historical figures, from King Solomon to George Washington Carver. The Reverend Brewster, already implicated in Civil Rights programs, began composing tunes like "Surely God is Able (to carry you through)" or "I'm Climbing Higher and Higher (and I won't come down)" that were meant to function as both gospel songs and codified political statements. In 1946, one of the most interesting mergers of gospel and politics occurred in New York City, at a concert, headlined by Paul Robeson, in honor of the left-wing Harlem congressman, Benjamin Davis. It featured the neo-jubilee quartet, the Harmonizing Four of Richmond, Virginia, Sister Rosa Shaw, one of the most daring if vocally limited improvisers in gospel history, the Two Gospel Keys, my own favorites of the so-called "downhome" singers, and a youthful quartet that included the brothers of James Baldwin, and an adolescent Clyde McPhatter. For many reasons, relating as much to politics as to the availability of talent, such a concert would be impossible today.

After 1945, with the advent of the small indenpendent companies—Savoy, Apollo, Gotham, Peacock, Specialty, Nashboro, etc.—gospel singers became recording stars. The tremendous increase in exposure and distribution facilitated gospel's new leap to prominence. During the next few years, groups like the Ward Singers, Davis Sisters, Roberta Martin Singers, and Original Gospel Harmonettes, and quartets like the Soul Stirrers, Pilgrim Travelers, Dixie Hummingbirds, and Five Blind Boys—to mention only the most popular acts—were met on the gospel highway by scores of gifted soloists and groups. These artists were largely sustained by their love of the music—even at gospel's peak, the average member of a big name group was lucky to clear $5000 a year. Despite inflation, this figure is not considerably larger today, although the segregated hotels and facilities that made life so unpleasant on the forties and fifties gospel highway are now gone. By the early fifties, it was clear that the best gospel singers had vocal and performing styles quite as distinctive as any found among jazz or blues vocalists. They also exhibited an infectious showmanship, a newer form of "clowning," that involved walking, running, or crawling up church aisles, and strutting and dancing with uninhibited gusto, and dramatic pantomimes: "painting a picture" to "tell a story." The quartets, the latest to jump on the gospel train, now assumed an easy mastery of the vocal and choreographic forms; they also continued to favor ballads that resembled the more maudlin rhythm and blues tunes of the time. Meanwhile crooners like Robert Anderson and Charles Watkins, and some of the more subdued female stylists like Lula Reed and Wynona Carr, both of whom later switched to rock and roll, were recording tunes that sounded, as church people said, "just like the blues" or at least like popular music. (And occasionally vice versa, as well, as when Marie Knight cut "Tell Me Why," a pop ballad to the tune of "Just a Closer Walk with Thee.")

The only gospel singer with whom white America was familiar during the 1950s was Mahalia Jackson. And although Jackson continued to shout her home congregation with classic versions of Brewster tunes like "Move On Up a Little Higher" and "How I Got Over," she made her mark with white audiences and critics, performing such uneventful material as "When the Saints Go Marching In" or "The Lord's Prayer." Yet gospel was having an oblique influence on general audiences. This came through the mimicry of gospel devices by the seminal singers in rock and roll. With the exception of Chuck Berry and Fats Domino, there is scarcely a pioneer rock and roll singer who didn't owe his stuff to the great gospel lead singers. These connections are very specific, though seldom noted, and a source of frequent discontent to the singers who can hardly accuse another person of plagiarism because he mimics their characteristic phrasing or vocal coloration. Sam Cooke, the successor to R. H. Harris with the Soul Stirrers, carried his own style and Harris's into rock and roll and had a singular influence on almost all subsequent soul crooners. Little Richard derived his falsetto whoops and growling syncopations, as well as his Suzy-Qs and hip-struts, from Marion Williams; and through Little Richard, his fellow Georgians, James Brown and Otis Redding, absorbed Williams's habits of rhythmic freedom and staccato word repetitions. Ray Charles seems to have had no one major influence, though his early "I've Got a Woman" derives from the Southern Tones's "It Must Be Jesus," his "Lonely Avenue" from the Pilgrim Travelers's "I've Got a New Home," and his "This Little Girl of Mine" from the Caravans's "What Kind of Man is This." Both Brook Benton and Jackie Wilson learned from Ira Tucker of the Dixie Hummingbirds. The Isley Brothers's "Shout" was a conscious homage, again, to Marion Williams, and contained an instrumental passage by the Apollo Theater's resident gospel organist, Professor Herman Stevens. Even B. B. King attempted a more florid approach than previous blues singers—in his case, colored largely by the example of the Reverend

Sam McCrary of the Fairfield Four. Wilson Pickett, in soul as earlier in gospel, is clearly indebted to the shouting vocal style and frenetic choreography of the Reverend Julius Cheeks. By the late fifties, rhythm and blues singers had expropriated the styles of many prominent gospel leads.

In a more tepid fashion, white singers followed suit. Elvis Presley, for one, had attended the Reverend Brewster's church in Memphis; even before, he had heard the popular records by Sister Rosetta Tharpe, accompanied by Sammy Price's boogie woogie trio, that captivated both black and white Southerners. There were even fifties recordings in the gospel style by Frankie Laine and Kay Starr; hardly soul-stirring, but a good deal less embarrassing than the recent attempts at hard gospel by folk-rockers.

How did gospel singers respond to this secularization of their sound? Not surprisingly, with confusion. The Gospel All Stars turned Ray Charles's "Hallelujah, I Love Her So" into "That's Why I Love Him So." The Davis Sisters had a hit in "There's a Tree on Each Side of the River" with its innovative, "ohh-wah" chorus: when they followed up with a tune that incorporated "she-bop-a-she-bop," the church audiences abandoned them. On the other hand, James Cleveland has been the biggest gospel star since 1960. His first hit, "The Love of God," was also the first gospel choir adaptation of a quasi-pop ballad, this one introduced by the Soul Stirrers, then led by their current crooner, Johnny Taylor, who was soon to become yet another gospel expatriate. In the late 1970s, Cleveland had big hits with gospel adaptations of pop ballads like "You're the Best Thing That Ever Happened to Me" and "I Write the Songs," a modern variant, if you will, of the old preacher ploy of one-upping the world with its own sentiments.

The Civil Rights movement was frequently accompanied by gospel songs, their latent content now made manifest. But a less happy trend was the popularity in the sixties of so-called "message" songs. Gospel singers performed them, in hopes

Secularization of Black Gospel Music

that the religiously neutral messages might remove the sting of their more sanctified performances. Yet, when one thinks of message tunes like the Staple Singers's "Respect Yourself" with its inane couplet—"keep talking 'bout the president, won't stop air pollution,/Put your hand on your mouth when you cough, that'll help the solution"—the descent in such tunes from the Reverend Brewster's apocalyptic imagery becomes the musical equivalent of the constricting of revolutionary ardor to reformist smugness. Well into the mid-seventies, gospel leads set the standards for soul and pop singers. Melismatics, falsetto shrieks, growls, simulated ecstacy became commonplace devices. The most important soul singer, Aretha Franklin drew on several sources—Mahalia Jackson, Jacqui Verdell, Mavis Staples, Marion Williams—though her prime influence has always been Clara Ward whose resonant moan continues to inform her style. Al Green owes his wispy falsetto flights to the Reverend Claude Jeter, former lead of the Swan Silvertones. Even Donna Summer hails Mahalia Jackson as her inspiration, though you couldn't prove it by me. I suspect Summer is talking like all those nondescript chanteuses who used to cite Ella Fitzgerald or Billie Holiday as their models. Certainly the extravagant gospel manner seems singularly unsuited to disco where it comes across either as overkill or as a contradiction in terms with the music.

In 1969, the first and only gospel record to hit the pop ten was released—the Edwin Hawkins Singers's "O Happy Day." With this record, the dominance of the so-called "contemporary" or "progressive" choir sound was assured. Fifties-style gospel did not disappear, but now found itself regarded as dated. The eclecticism of "contemporary gospel" derives from several sources: the academic training of many young choir directors; the example of the highly complex recording techniques of a Stevie Wonder or Michael Jackson; and the simple financial lure. Although at this moment, most gospel singers are as badly off as ever, the four or five top names are charging between five and ten thousand dollars per concert.

A typical, contemporary choir recording may be all over the musical terrain—with melodies that evoke soul ballads, high church anthems, and themes out of Wagner or Brahms, with harmonies that give the contemporary part singer the pleasure of singing augmented fifths and diminished sevenths, with rhythms that merge church and discotheque, and polyrhythms supplied by cantilevered and intersecting choral lines, as well as piano, organ, rhythm instruments, and even synthesizers. The results are seldom successful. Yet the boldness of the attempt is in that gospel tradition that has always accommodated daring improvisations and vocal risks, applauding most recently male sopranos and female basses.

Gospel choirs may have dropped much of the content, but they retain the familiar forms of gospel worship. The choir lead will frequently retard a complicated tempo to the atemporal pace of a Dr. Watts hymn. Choir members are extravagant shouters; frequently an entire choir will dance; and the ensuing displays, idiosyncratic and self-absorbed, put to shame the secularized corybants of most discos. Spirit feel yet obtains; songs still go on for half an hour, when the spirit is ripe. And surely if these ambitious choir directors had access to rock recording budgets, the results would be happier. The average gospel album is recorded in four to six hours, with budgets below five thousand dollars. Though young peoples' choirs are training young musicians to provide self-contained recording ensembles, in many cases, the rule is, as a witty disc jockey put it, "We're recording tonight. Bring your mother; we heard she plays piano."

Paradoxically, as contemporary gospel choirs sound more and more like worldly music, white pop singers continue to use traditional gospel backups. Post-Beatles rock musicians may have determined to combine all the musical sounds at their disposal; actually they have profited at the expense of almost all the older forms they have exploited. In rock, gospel had been reduced to a vocal coloration, usually in the background, represented by overly fervent, high pitched singers. Properly they should call attention to the vocal inadequacies of a Bob Dylan or Paul Simon, but I fear that they wind up sounding naive and ingenuous, temperamentally limited unlike the genial parodists they support.

There have been other dubious uses of gospel. It is currently employed in the lecture-services of the Reverend Jesse Jackson; last summer, at a low point in the polls, Jimmy Carter brought some gospel singers to the White House, desperate for any constituency; Andrae Crouch, a leading gospel singer, appeared recently on the Grammy Awards television broadcast and thanked "your forefathers for telling my forefathers that Jesus is Lord." And then there is the current prominence of two white evangelical television programs, the 700 Club and the P. T. L. Club, with their combinations of extreme right wing politics and the more forbidding forms of American evangelism. Today, despite studio audiences that are usually 99 percent white, they provide the only televised forums for black gospel singers, and a common gospel aspiration is to appear on them, sandwiched between the likes of Anita Bryant and Senator Jesse Helms.

The old gospel sound, however, has not disappeared. Though during the seventies, Mahalia Jackson, Clara Ward, Brother Joe May, Rosetta Tharpe, and Alex Bradford all died, there are still many gospel giants around, including such old-timers as Thomas A. Dorsey, the Reverend Brewster, Willie Mae Ford Smith, and Sallie Martin. The gospel blues is not an exhausted form; in fact, there are far more blues-imbued recordings released annually in gospel than in soul music. There are still downhome, regional artists and virtuoso musicians, including a recent blossoming of saxophonists. John Hammond once said that gospel singers have nine lives—some of the best may seem to have sold out for good, and then manage to reassert their power when one least expects it. The world has come close to defeating gospel music, the bad times swamping the good news, but as a recent gospel hit declared, "I don't feel no ways tired, I've come too far from where I started"; the spirit's still there, the battle isn't over.

PART IV

Pure Country

Honky Tonk: The Music of the Southern Working Class

Bill Malone

I left my home down on a rural route[1]
And told my mom I'm going stepping out,
To get the honky tonk blues.

THE COUNTRY CHURCH, the county schoolhouse, the village barn dance, and the family parlor all occupy honored places in the history of country music as shaping forces in the evolution of the genre. All of them mirror the pastoral origins of country music, just as their continued emphasis in written accounts reflects a rural bias on the part of scholars. The honky tonk, on the other hand, which Hank Williams described in the above song, has been anything but pastoral, but it may have been the most powerful influence yet. Since antiquity a powerful interrelationship between drinking and musical entertainment has existed, and the tavern, or its equivalent, has always played an important role in the dissemination of music. But as a force for musical change in country music, its history properly begins in the thirties. It was then that the combined forces of prohibition repeal and increased commercialization and professionalization in the still new hillbilly music field led to the movement of musicians into the taverns and beer joints where their music was welcomed. When country music entered the honky tonks, its performing styles and its thematic content changed significantly. Much of that story I have told elsewhere.[2] My chief focus in this paper, however, will be on the years since World War II when the music of the honky tonk became, at least for a time, virtually *the* sound of country music, as well as the most valid expression in song of the world view of the Southern working class.

If the thirties were important as years of nourishment, the war years were absolutely indispensable in both the maturation and popularization of honky tonk music. Like no other phenomenon before it, the war contributed to the weakening of the agricultural nexus and the subsequent migration of people into towns and industrial cities of the South, as well as into cities in the Midwest and on the West Coast. While rural civilians changed their locales and their occupations, their military sons and daughters moved to training camps both in and out of the South and to combat theatres around the world. For a people in transition, who were now urban in residence but yet rural in style and outlook, the adjustment was often fraught with frustration and pain: housing was both inadequate and scarce; work was plentiful but fraught with an unfamiliar regimentation; and family solidarity was weakened by a whole host of complex urban problems, not the least of which was the growing entry of women into the work force, and the increased availability of alternative role models for youth. In that time of stress people tended to seek security in that which was familiar. Women, for example, often sought the solace of religion (probably to a greater extent than men), and radio evangelists and charismatic tent revivalists found a large and enthusiastic audience among Southerners in the late 1940s. For men the pressures and frustrations of city life could be especially traumatic, and the threats to masculine supremacy, already strongly present in rural life, were made even more glaring in the newly adopted urban milieu. Many men, and their sons (but, it is hoped, not their daughters), sought to reaffirm their identities in a sympathetic setting: over a bottle of beer in a honky tonk.

The honky tonk[3] was a man's world. Although women were sought there, it was not considered their domain, and those who entered were not respected. Men might accompany their wives or girlfriends to a dance, but the unattached "honky tonk angel" was both a lure and a threat. While she tempted, she also reminded one of that potential in all women, and was a premonition of the liberation that was soon to come. Men went to honky tonks for the widest variety of reasons, and as both casual and serious drinkers. Many who frequented honky tonks during the war years, whether industrial laborer or serviceman, were gripped by a sense of isolation—the loneliness that came from social displacement or from the physical separation from loved ones. The lonely drinker sought communion with the bottle, his companion on the nearby barstool, and the music of the jukebox. The music of the honky tonks, whether live or on jukeboxes, reflected increasingly the preoccupation of these displaced ruralites. Furthermore, a body of songs about the honky tonk world itself, and about the experience of entertainers who appeared there, began to comprise a significant portion of the country music repertory. Rustic sounds still thrived in country music during the forties; the decade, after all, marked the heyday of mountain singer Roy Acuff. But styles born in the honky tonks of Texas predominated, and names like Bob Wills, Ted Daffan, Floyd Tillman, Moon Mullican, Cliff Bruner, and Al Dexter dominated the jukeboxes. Al Dexter's "Pistol Packin' Mama," a giant hit of 1943, and an example of the rollicking side of honky tonk, was inspired by its singer-composer's experiences in the oil town-honky tonk atmosphere of Texas in the thirties (the story grew out of an incident witnessed by Dexter in a Longview dancehall). Voicing the cry-in-your-beer side of honky tonk, almost to the point of suicidal impulse, were such songs as Rex Griffin's "The Last Letter," Ted Daffan's "Born to Lose," and Floyd Tillman's "It Makes No Difference Now," which poured forth from a thousand jukeboxes and were carried around the world by lonely and homesick

Southern servicemen. When Ernest Tubb moved to the Grand Ole Opry in 1943, his Texas-born and beer-joint-nourished style gained a national forum. As he won disciples, the style he embodied insinuated itself into the music of country entertainers everywhere, from West Virginia to California.

The immediate years following World War II witnessed country music's first great commercial boom. Postwar prosperity created an audience that was eager for and receptive to commercial music diversion. The number of musicians, and the establishments receptive to their music, proliferated. Not all singers went willingly to the honky tonks. The honky tonk's reputation for violence comes more from this period than from any other. The threat to life and limb was as real for the entertainer as it was for the customer, as drunken oil field roughnecks or industrial workers playing cowboy worked out their fantasies or tested their macho impulses in the competitive arena of the barroom. For many young men a violent barroom encounter was a ritualized expression of manhood. For others it was a way of coping with the frustrations of boring, and generally low-paying, jobs. The stories may be apochryphal, but musicians still tell of playing on stages protected by chicken wire from flying beer bottles. Few entertainers have very pleasant memories about what Glen Campbell would later call the "fightin'-and-dancin' " clubs. The honky tonk circuit was a hard apprenticeship for country entertainers, but the styles developed there moved into the recording studios and the concert halls where they altered the whole sound and tone of American country music.

Honky tonk performance worked hand in hand with technological progress to encourage sophisticated innovations in instrumentation. Electric guitars, both standard and steel, became common in most country bands, and by 1954 the pedal steel guitar, a basic ingredient of honky tonk instrumentation, and probably the closest thing yet to an approximation of the vocal honky tonk whine, had been introduced (first on Webb Pierce's recording of "Slowly"). The honky tonk style never exercised a complete monopoly (Eddy Arnold's successful sound of the mid-forties embodied a composite of influences), but, for all practical purposes, it had become the all-pervasive sound of mainstream country music. The typical band was small and featured a fiddle, a steel guitar and "takeoff" guitar (both electrified), string bass, a rhythm guitar played in "sock", or percussive, style, occasionally a piano, but almost never a drum. The musicians were capable of performing the hot instrumental licks pioneered by the Western swing bands of the thirties, but instrumentation was usually subordinated to the needs of a vocalist. A new generation of honky tonk singers had emerged, and some of them, like Hank Thompson, Webb Pierce, Lefty Frizzell, and Floyd Tillman[4], were among the most distinctive stylists that the country music field has seen.

Surpassing them all, however, was the immensely talented singer from Alabama, Hank Williams, whose style reflected the tensions that had produced the honky tonk genre, and whose career marked the greatest commercial flowering yet of the honky tonk style. Hank sang to an audience who, for better or worse, were having to come to terms with life in an industrial-urban environment. Adults might dream of the abandoned rural life, but few had thoughts about returning to it. Their children had no illusions about rural life, and they made up the bulk of country music's burgeoning audience in the early fifties. Very soon, the youngest of them would be lured away by the rollicking, and sensual, sounds of rock and roll, a style that would render honky tonk a strong and almost devastating blow. Hank Williams's career and style certainly do not totally embody the whole of country music history, but they epitomize a large slice of it. Reared in a fundamentalist, but violently unstable, religious atmosphere,[5] Williams was never able to rid himself of the influences learned there, both musical and doctrinal, and he took them into the honky tonks of south Alabama where he began singing by the time he was fourteen years old. Stylistically, his music represented a fusion of that of his two heroes, the Texas Ernest Tubb and the Tennesseean Roy Acuff (an example of similar amalgamations in the larger field of country music), and, thematically, his songs embodied the ambivalence that lay at the heart of Southern working class culture: hedonism and puritanism, machismo and sentimentality, sin and guilt. Williams and his audience interrelated with an intimacy that had hardly been equalled in country music's previous history, because culturally they were one.

When Hank Williams died in 1953, few could have anticipated that very soon the honky tonk style would be driven from recordings, and that the whole country music genre, which had thrived so mightily after the war, would be in shambles. The rock and roll phenomenon, which ironically derived much of its energy and stylistic traits from country music tradition (a fascination with boogie and "hot" rhythms often exhibited by earlier country musicians), was also a product of the urbanization process discussed earlier. The rock and roll wave inundated American music, and all forms of traditional country music were driven underground as promoters and recording men began their frantic searches for young and vigorous stylists who could recreate what Elvis had done and who could permanently hold that youthful audience that now dominated American music. The Nashville music industry responded to these challenges in a variety of ways, one of which was the production of a pop style of country music, known by such designations as "the Nashville Sound," "country pop," or "countrypolitan," which would allegedly preserve the ambience of older country music while building a new audience who preferred their music to be served up in less raw forms. For a brief period in the midfifties, fiddles and steel guitars almost disappeared from country recordings and from jukeboxes.

Honky tonk music, however, like bluegrass, did not vanish. Both forms went "underground," and honky tonk continued to thrive, especially in the clubs of Texas and

Southern California where veterans like Ernest Tubb, and newcomers like Willie Nelson, George Jones, Charlie Walker, and Wynn Stewart remained faithful to the beer-drinking style. One singer resisted both the rock and roll and country pop tides, and not only prospered with his version of the honky tonk genre, but introduced dynamic innovations which have influenced the field ever since. This was Ray Price, whose recording of "Crazy Arms" in 1956 successfully competed on the charts with country-pop tunes and ushered in a new and vital phase of honky tonk history. Price's band, the Cherokee Cowboys, were almost totally electrified (fiddles included); the electric bass had replaced the older standup instrument; and drums had become an integral aspect of this dancehall-oriented music. While the wailing pedal steel guitar and the heavily-bowed single-string-style fiddle took their lead passages, the drums and rhythm guitar set down a hard rhythm as the electric bass surrounded it all with walking bass patterns. This was the "Texas Shuffle Beat," an infectious dance style, and some of the best country music ever made.

Like his mentor, Hank Williams, before him, Price inspired a host of disciples. The Cherokee Cowboys's roster reads like a who's who of country music. At one time or another, the band included Johnny Bush, Roger Miller, Johnny Paycheck, Willie Nelson, Buddy Emmons, Tommy Jackson, and Buddy Spicher. By the beginning of the sixties these men had gone on to pursue their own careers, and many others, both within and outside the pale of Ray Price influence, had contributed to a honky tonk revival. George Jones, building on a long tenure in the southeast Texas dance halls of Beaumont, Port Arthur, Orange, and Houston, produced hit after hit as he became one of the supreme stylists of country music. Buck Owens, Texas-born, but a product of California's country ballroom scene, topped the charts in the early sixties with a supercharged instrumental style (part honky tonk, and part rockabilly) dominated by the sound of the pedal steel guitar.

Later in the decade another California-based singer, Merle Haggard, who is a rare breed, indeed, because he was born in the state, took the honky tonk style to even greater commercial heights with songs like "The Bottle Let Me Down" and "Swinging Doors." He and Loretta Lynn demonstrated in the late sixties and early seventies that it was possible to be both "hard country" and successful at the same time. It was a lesson readily absorbed by many young performers, but one from which the country music industry as a whole has profited little.

Honky tonk music, therefore, revived with new strength from its doldrums of the mid-fifties. The style, though, has never since predominated as it did in the early fifties and will probably never do so again. The country music industry has prospered to an extent never thought possible back during the rock and roll period, and the Nashville facet of the industry, absorbed with self-image, has attempted to be "all things to all people." Country music has simultaneously identified with Middle America, the working man, and progressive youth, while also reaching out for that affluent middle class audience which is presumably different from the other three categories. In an industry obsessed with "crossovers," the hard honky tonk sound is unwelcomed; indeed, it is embarrassing. Furthermore, the temptation among performers to cross over to the more lucrative and respectable pop country field is almost irresistible. Singers experiment with the honky tonk field, as in the case of Johnny Rodriguez and his initial recording of "Pass Me By," but soon move into other stylistic categories. A few, like Ronnie Milsap, Jerry Lee Lewis, and Hank Williams, Jr., demonstrate a mastery of the honky tonk style, when they choose to do so; but that choice is made infrequently. For a singer to perform consistently in the honky tonk vein is rare; for one to prosper doing so is even more unusual. Ernest Tubb still makes between 200 and 300 personal appearances a year. His audience is large and loyal, but it has also been with him for probably thirty years. Other singers, like Norman Wade, Vernon Oxford, and Boxcar Willie, project sounds, and often songs that come directly out of the fifties. And there are probably a thousand others much like them in a thousand honky tonks throughout America, unnoticed and unknown anywhere outside their own locales, who still remain true to visions cast long ago by Ernest, Lefty, or Hank. The singers who have done most to preserve the honky tonk style, while at the same time creating identities apart from earlier models, are Gene Watson, John Anderson, and above all, Moe Bandy (born in Meridian, Mississippi, but reared, biologically and musically, in San Antonio, Texas). Bandy probably does not deserve to be called "the Jesus Christ of country music," as Nick Tosches has termed him, but his clean, crisp articulation of lyrics dealing with drinking, cheating, and heartbreak, performed with a backdrop of fiddle and pedal guitar, cuts like a breath of fresh air through the fetid morass of country pop.

This essay began with the argument that honky tonk was once the sound of mainstream country music. It concludes by arguing that, while it no longer predominates, it now represents the best in a music that is losing its soul. Honky tonk music, unlike other country styles, has been hampered less by artificiality. It has not consciously tried to preserve or recreate (as has bluegrass), nor has it reached out to build a new audience. Of all country music styles it has been the closest organic reflection of Southern working class culture, and the one that most closely marks the evolution of the Southern folk from rural to urban-industrial life. Although intimately tied to the urban adjustment of Southern plain folk, it has been ignored by folklorists because it is not pastoral, and because it does not protest. It is scorned by the country music industry because it is too country. And it is dismissed by many of us, I am convinced, because it is too real. Honky tonk instrumentation both attracts and repels: to many of us, the whine of the pedal steel guitar and bounce of the shuffle beat evoke elemental, and often cathartic, impulses and emotions.

To others, they undoubtedly conjure up distasteful seamy and seedy images. The lyrics and instrumentation of honky tonk music combine to evoke a side of human nature that we do not always like to see, or at least do not like to recognize: a vision of emotional pain and isolation and human weakness that we have all shared. The lyrics may be too revealing emotionally to accept intellectually. At their worst, the songs can be so full of trite self-pity as to drown us in their bathos. But at their best, songs like "Borrowed Angel," "Who'll Turn Out the Lights," or George Jones's marvelously-performed "The Grand Tour," speak to the loneliness, and the need for human empathy in each of us.

[1] Hank Williams, "Honky Tonk Blues." The orally-delivered paper was illustrated with relevant recordings. These included Floyd Tillman, "Slipping Around," Ernest Tubb, "Walking the Floor Over You," Ray Price, "Crazy Arms," Stoney Edwards, "Old Hank and Lefty Raised My Country Soul," Moe Bandy, "It Was Always So Easy (to Find an Unhappy Woman)," and George Jones, "The Grand Tour."

[2] The first history and analysis of honky tonk as a subgenre of country music appeared in my doctoral dissertation, "A History of Commercial Country Music in the United States, 1920-1964" (University of Texas, Austin, 1964), and in my subsequent book, *Country Music, USA* (Austin: University of Texas Press, for the American Folklore Society, 1968). Another analysis of the phenomenon, along with recorded examples, is found in *The Smithsonian Collection of Classic Country Music* (organized and edited by Bill C. Malone, 1981).

[3] The term "honky tonk" probably has urban black origins, but by the 1930s it had come to be identified with roadhouses generally frequented by Southern whites. Honky tonks were usually located on the outskirts of town, partly because of the quest for reduced legal surveillance and for low tax rates, but also because of the county option policy favored by such states as Texas. Honky tonks often operated near the county lines in order to draw clientele from both wet and dry counties. With the passage of time, "honky tonk" became virtually a generic term for any establishment which sold beer, permitted dancing, and featured country music.

[4] Floyd Tillman had been an active participant in the Texas honky tonk scene since about 1935, as both a singer and sideman, but he did not become known as a solo singing star until after 1949.

[5] The best account of Williams's early life and influences is Chet Flippo, *Your Cheatin' Heart* (New York: Simon and Schuster, 1981).

Commercialization and Tradition in the Nashville Sound

William Ivey

THE ENTIRE QUESTION OF TRADITION and its ability to survive in a contemporary urban context has certainly been of major significance to American folklorists. As filmmaker Jean Renoir stated, "It is practically the only question of the age, this question of primitivism and how it can be sustained in the face of sophistication." Folklorists have answered this question in a variety of ways, and I will not digress by restating Richard Dorson's arguments for relating folklore to the American Experience, nor will I present the work of contextualists or the more recent argument (formulated rather opaquely in Del Hymes's unfairly ignored American Folklore Society presidential address) that the need to "traditionalize" some part of group experience is a kind of cultural universal. I will only stress that because folklorists are drawn by temperament to those arts and artifacts that seem to reflect specific cultures rather directly (and country music is certainly one of those arts) the shifting moods of folklore scholarship, the changing definitions of "traditional" and "commercial," form an inevitable backdrop to a discussion of country music in general and the "Nashville Sound" in particular.

Within folk music study scholars have been particularly interested in questions of transmission, textual analysis, and in a general sense, with questions of authenticity, which frequently equals questions of quality. This latter interest has resulted in the development of certain perceived continuums that help to locate a particular performance in relation to its degree of folkness or degree of authenticity, perhaps on a scale of one to ten. If you drew such a horizontal scale for blues you would, I suppose, locate Robert Johnson at the "very traditional" end of the scale with a rating of nine or ten and an artist like Stevie Wonder near the other end of the scale with a rating of one or two. Much of black musical expression could be located between these two extremes.

The same kind of scale can be drawn for country music, with early string band music and balladry on record at one end of the scale, and with, let's say, Anne Murray or Kenny Rogers at the other end of the scale—or perhaps just off the scale.

However, as observers of what is traditional in culture our attitudes shift. For some, use of electric instruments indicated a clear decline in "traditionality" of an item or style. That's no longer true. Among other factors, a little distance in time from a given popular culture item allows us to see more clearly its "traditional" component.

It is important to note that many scholars see the popular or commercial elements in these musical traditions as hostile to, or even destructive of, the elements identified with a pure oral tradition. There have been countless allusions through the years to the destructive impact of popular or commercial art upon folk art— they need not be restated here. This pervasive view of popular culture as negative and destructive has produced a shorthand stereotype of commercial music which sees it as the functional antitheses of traditional music, and so we see that—to use the example of country music—balladry and string band music of the twenties possesses the virtue of oral tradition (amateur, community oriented, culturally reinforcing, local, expressive of community values) while the Nashville Sound is commercial, national, imposed upon communities, reflective of industry perceptions of what will sell, and impersonal. I wish to restate this admittedly overdrawn characterization of attitudes toward the role of commercial forces in traditional music only to suggest that we may now possess a less-than-complete view of these commercial forms, a less-than-thorough understanding of their functional role in the adaptation of rural traditions to urban life and contemporary technology.

The phrase "Nashville Sound" means several different things, and it is worthwhile to briefly describe each of these meanings. The origins of the phrase are obscure, but it was fixed in popular culture by a *Time* magazine story in 1963, and by the late 1960s was being reinforced by a major record company as RCA noted each country album as "recorded in RCA's Nashville Sound studio."

First, the "Nashville Sound" refers to an era in which country music responded to pressures and demands of the marketplace in order to carve a permanent niche within the larger popular music spectrum in the United States. The era of the Nashville Sound began in 1957 with the formation of the Country Music Association (CMA) and the development of a broad strategy directed toward recovering markets lost during the rock and roll surge of the mid-1950s. Though some observers have described this effort in nearly conspiratorial terms, it was, in fact, a rather loose effort with several rather ill-defined goals. The first observable purpose of CMA's program was to increase the number of radio stations programming country records; a second and related goal was the establishment of country music as a commercially viable entity, that is, as a product which could, by association, be used to sell other products. This second effort demanded a direct approach to account executives with major advertising agencies, and this was accomplished in a New York country showcase in 1963, and through a widely distributed promotional film entitled *For My Next Number* produced by CMA in 1970. This assault upon advertising did increase the appeal of country stations to advertisers. Advertising rates for country stations increased and the country format became increasingly attractive (and profitable) to radio station management. For more than ten years following the organization of CMA, the number of country radio stations increased steadily and dramatically, and the effort was labeled a great success within the industry.

Now the music itself changed during this same period (roughly 1957 to 1971), partly through a natural evolutionary process and partly in response to the same forces which created CMA and its drive to increase the availability of country music on radio. Much has been made of the addition of certain cliches of pop music—sight-reading string and horn sections and background vocal groups—to country recording during this period. This graft of pop sophistication onto country performance style is the second meaning given the phrase "the Nashville Sound," and is undoubtedly the aspect most frequently cited as hostile to authentic, traditional, mainstream country music, and recordings by Jim Reeves, Eddy Arnold, Patsy Cline, and Marty Robbins are trotted out to reveal the depths to which country performance style had sunk under the weight of commercialization.

No doubt part of the changes in country style in the late 1950s and early 1960s were the result of commercial forces at work; however, these changes also possessed a rather spontaneous quality, and were in some ways quite independent of the marketing strategy organized by the Country Music Association. The principals in the evolution of this particular aspect of the Nashville Sound—record producers Owen Bradley, Chet Atkins and Don Law—were by experience and musical temperament inclined toward popular music and away from the primitive ruralisms of "hillbilly" tradition. Bradley had been a society band leader in Nashville before his emergence as Decca's chief country A & R man. Though Chet Atkins possessed impeccable credentials as a rural folk, his wide experience as a radio sideman, his interest in many different styles of music, and his intense feelings of inferiority surrounding his childhood led him away from his roots as a string-band fiddler. Law also brought sophisticated, urban musical tastes to his role as A & R chief for Columbia. In addition, Atkins, Law and Bradley used the Nashville Sound to break free of New York control. Thus, given the interests of these three leading record producers (and the three account for such careers as those of Don Gibson, Eddy Arnold, Jim Reeves, Patsy Cline, Brenda Lee, Marty Robbins and Sonny James), it is likely that country music would have taken a firm jog in the direction of popular performance style in the late 1950s even if industry demands for discs with broad audience appeal had not permeated the Nashville music community.

What I've just said about the Nashville Sound is really prologue to the particular meaning of the phrase that interests me and that I would like to examine in some detail today. This third use of the phrase is somewhat more technical and musicological than the meanings already considered, but I think this use of the term sheds a certain positive light on this era in the development of country music. Much discussion of the Nashville Sound stresses the first and second meanings of the phrase and gives only the most cursory examination of the sound itself—those elements that provided Nashville recordings with a distinctive character in the years between 1957 and 1971. In fact, virtually all that has been written refers to the echo, background vocal groups, string sections and so on—the graft of pop cliches onto country music. However, I would argue that there was a distinctive sound produced in Nashville studios during the years in question, that it can be described and analyzed, that it developed its own musical and non-musical "traditions," and that it can be viewed as a very positive step in the accomodation between commercial sophistication and primitive traditional art.

The key to the meaing of the phrase "the Nashville Sound" is found in the work of Nashville studio musicians, the development of a particular standard instrumentation for country music, the evolution of a particular style of notation for use in studios and the development of specific techniques of personal interaction compatible with country music, musicians, and country singers.

Here are some of the features that characterize the Nashville Sound: the use of relatively small ensembles with an emphasis on fretted stringed instruments (as many as six guitars of one sort or another on each session); the development of "head" arrangements on the spot during a recording session, and the use of a notation system developed to meet the needs of "by ear" musicians and improvisatory arrangements; a standard of instrumental performance that subordinates instrumentation to vocal performance, an approach to recording that stands in contrast to the "wall of sound" techniques evident in many mainstream pop records of the 1950s and 1960s. The Nashville Sound further aimed at developing a relaxed sound and achieved this goal by consistently maintaining an informal "we're just a bunch of good ole boys having a good time" attitude in the recording studio. Finally the Nashville Sound was characterized by the emergence of several "teams" of musicians accustomed to working together and capable of moving from studio to studio developing interesting on-the-spot arrangements on short notice.

It seems very clear to me that the elements I have just described (and some, of course, are non-musical aspects of performance style) are those of genuine substance—the elements that, in the late 1960s, drew performers like Bob Dylan and Joan Baez and others to Nashville studios. In the years between 1957 and 1971 these elements of recording technique formed the foundation of Nashville musicianship, and even when combined with such obvious bows to pop music as string sections and vocal groups (and significantly this section work was often overdubbed after the "core" musicians and vocalist had recorded their tracks) the approach provided Nashville records with a sound which was internationally admired and ultimately much imitated.

The standard "core" instrumentation of Nashville Sound recording sessions was basically composed of rhythm-section instruments with a strong emphasis on guitars. Typical instrumentation was acoustic bass, drums, piano, one or two rhythm guitars played in an "open" style, electric lead guitar, bass guitar (the six-stringed instrument used only in Nashville in these years, tuned an octave above a double bass and an octave below a standard guitar), pedal steel guitar, and, fairly often, the fiddle. During the fifties and sixties much of this instrumentation was unique to the Nashville recording scene. The six-string electric bass has never been utilized anywhere else, and both the pedal steel and two open rhythm guitars (one rhythm guitar tuned with octave strings) had not yet been exported from Nashville to the larger national and international recording industry. Instrumentation alone was enough to provide a distinct Nashville Sound in this era.

A unique instrumentation was supported by a distinctive approach to creating arrangements, adding to the substance of the Nashville Sound. Arrangements were frequently sparse. The bass drum was little used, and instrumental solo lines were employed sparingly. It is a principle of Nashville recording that only one instrument plays prominently at any one time, and the possible roles available to individual instruments were rather limited—they were, in fact, pretty much restricted to the "backing," "filling," and "soloing" roles outlined years ago by Mayne Smith in his pioneering description of bluegrass performance style.

The result of these techniques and this instrumentation was a relatively sparse sound, one which clearly remained subordinate to the work of the lead vocalist. This stated goal of staying out of the way of the lyric and the vocalist stood in contrast to the heavily arranged, heavily instrumented recordings then associated with mainstream popular music (Tony Bennett, Frank Sinatra, today Barbra Streisand), but was, of course, compatible with the emphasis on lyric long associated with country music.

Though instruments were employed with considerable restraint within the recording center, it should not be assumed that there existed little opportunity for the exercise of individual creativity on the part of Nashville studio musicians. The approach to recording in this period allowed musicians great latitude in determining what specific lines would be played by which instruments at which particular moment in a performance. Musicians were also encouraged to create "hooks" or "gimmicks" which might help set a record apart and assist it in gaining radio air play and commercial success. The descending dobro line in "Harper Valley PTA," the fuzz-tone guitar in Marty Robbins's "Don't Worry," and the clink of the hammer on steel in Jimmie Dean's "Big John" are examples of instrumental "licks" created on the spot during recording sessions by studio musicians, and each contributed significantly to the popularity of those recordings.

A recording system in which the instrumentalists rarely read standard notation and a system in which arrangers were relegated to the pedestrian task of arranging strings and horns for overdub sessions allowed the creative impulses of studio musicians to escape with some regularity. This ability to draw on the talents of many musicians on short notice was probably the key factor which attracted so many pop artists to Nashville studios during the 1960s.

One final element must be considered in a close look at the makeup of the Nashville Sound. It is a subtle point, but one which, I think, comes close to integrating our perception of a specific era of Nashville recording with Del Hymes's argument for the universality of the need to traditionalize experience. Richard A. Peterson and Howard G. White in a fascinating article in the periodical *Urban Life* examine in some detail the social structure of studio musicianship. Though their broad goal is to outline a general "simplex" structure applicable to any informal association of artists, the evidence presented takes us a final step in our journey to flesh out the real meaning of the phrase "the Nashville Sound." Peterson and White list those factors which allow a studio musician to fit in with his or her fellow practitioners. Among the attributes are technical competence, social reliability, a craftsmanlike bearing (the appearance of competence), a willingness to do what is, technically, illegal work and, finally, the studio musician must participate in an overall occupational ideology of craftsmanship, an ideology which, for example, defines creativity "not in terms of the egoistic self-expression of genius, but as the ability to understand and deliver on demand exactly what is required."

These attributes, all but one of which have little to do with a musician's ability to play, reached a particularly high level of development in Nashville, because the absence of written arrangements allowed this "ability to deliver on demand" to flourish.

Peterson and White continue to analyze the web of ideology, rumor, custom, dress, and intrigue that unify studio musicians within a particular environment. In the descriptive process they make a strong case for studio musicians as an occupational group with particularly strong and diverse folkways which unite them and separate them from other groups.

My point here has been that there is a great deal of interest within the distinctive musical style, identified as the Nashville Sound. The music had a distinct approach to recording—one not all that incompatible with country recording of earlier eras. The music was in no way the mere obverse of traditional country music—a gloss of pop cliches spread over the last evolutionary stage of a dying traditional form. In fact, the most frequently cited excesses of the era—string and horn sections, background vocals—were themselves merely incidental add-ons to what was a dynamic, definable approach to recording. The obvious excesses of the Nashville Sound have earned criticisms, but it was the significant core— the relaxed studio environment, the lack of written arrangements, the evolution of creative teams of studio musicians, the utilization of a specific cluster of stringed instruments—that so attracted performers from outside the recognized boundaries of country music.

I speak of the music in the past tense and, for several reasons, I am convinced that the Nashville Sound is dead or nearly so. It peaked in 1971 (I personally think it peaked with Sammi Smith's recording of "Help Me Make It Through the Night") and from that time forward it fell into repetition and self-imitation. For one thing, the same teams of musicians got all the jobs and, therefore, weren't so creative. Also by the middle 1970s the Austin-based Outlaw Movement was creating a back-to-basics trend within country music. However, some of the most important attributes of the form—pedal steel guitar work, the uncluttered sound, the "laid back" drumming, the head arrangements—were quickly adopted by other recording centers. By 1975 a performer could cut a record in Los Angeles, New York, or London and have it emerge in perfect emulation of the Nashville Sound. In 1975 country music's biggest record was John Denver's "Back Home Again." This ushered in the era of Olivia Newton John and Linda Ronstadt; an era of Nashville-style records cut in other places.

I think it was a great era in the adaptation of one minority music to the forces of a national popular culture. As we look more closely at the components of the Nashville Sound, it, too, will gradually fade into the warm glow of sentiment and respect now reserved for old-time, western swing, bluegrass and honky tonk style.

PART V

Myths and Heroes

Charles Ives: Victorian Gentleman or American Folk Hero?

Vivian Perlis

THERE IS AN AIR OF MYSTERY about Charles Ives, an unsolved riddle, an enigma. This is surprising, considering Ives was a contemporary figure—he lived until 1954, and there are still people alive who remember him and who worked directly with him. Ives's life, his music, and his place in twentieth-century history have been closely examined in several substantial books and articles; he has been the subject of an extensive oral history project[1] and a documentary television drama.[2] Yet it is almost more difficult to describe Ives than Mozart or Beethoven. A look at the Ives picture reveals not a precise portrait, but a Picasso-like duality which can be both frustrating and fascinating for biographers and historians. The causes behind this out-of-focus picture have to do with paradoxes and inconsistencies in Ives's life and music. Ironically, it is one consistent trait in Ives—his overwhelming respect and desire for personal privacy—that contributes in great part to the aura of secrecy surrounding him. While the theme of artistic isolation is not a new one in the arts, it is less acceptable in our media-dominated society where culture idols are expected to be open and accessible—one thinks, for example, of Norman Mailer and Leonard Bernstein. However, one of the paradoxes in Ives is that he could be both ultra-modern and terribly old-fashioned, way ahead of his time and far behind it. Loneliness, solitariness, and hard work were virtues to Ives, and what could be acquired, perceived, or understood easily was suspect. It is doubtful that Ives made a conscious attempt to be difficult and evasive to historians, as he did to photographers in his lifetime, but it is safe to assume that he would not have wanted to be neatly pinned down and categorized. And so, despite the documentation, including Ives's own voluminous writings and correspondence,[3] the questions persist. How could this financially successful insurance executive be the most innovative American composer of the century? How was it that the great idealist with such advanced ideas of social and political reform lived as he did—with a city and country home, cars, and servants? Was Charles Ives a revolutionary or a patriot? Millionaire or socialist? Amateur musician or avant-garde leader? Gentleman or folk hero?

Ives, Victorian Gentleman

William Ives, captain of the ship *Truelove*, was the first American ancestor of Charles Ives. He brought settlers from England to Boston in 1635, and then to New Haven in 1638. According to a cousin of Ives, Amelia Van Wyck, "The Ives family was one of the oldest and best in New England."[4] Charles was the first-born of Mary Parmelee and George Ives, bandmaster of Danbury, Connecticut. Young Charlie learned music from his father. He grew up on Bach and Beethoven, studied organ, and became the youngest professional organist in the state at age thirteen. That same year, Ives wrote his first piece, *Holiday Quickstep*. At sixteen, Ives composed a set of variations on *America*—today, in an orchestral arrangement by William Schuman, the most often performed work by any American composer. Ives attended Danbury Academy, Danbury High School, and Hopkins Preparatory. Far better known as an athlete than a musician, young Ives achieved fame as captain of the football team that beat Yale's freshman squad. When Ives entered Yale in 1894, he was handsome, fun-loving, athletic, and only passably good at his courses. In short, he was a typical turn-of-the-century Yalie. Before long he joined a fraternity and was tapped for a secret society. Ives was not political. Ives was not radical. Ives made no trouble of any kind. When Professor Horatio Parker, the highly respected conservative composer advised Ives "not to hog all the keys at one meal," Charlie quietly kept his more adventurous music out of the classroom, and when Parker requested that he change the ending of the first movement of the *First Symphony*, Ives did so in order to complete his graduation requirements. The symphony is a big romantic work without innovations. As expected of a Yale man after graduation, Ives decided to go into business. He joined several other graduates in a sprawling New York apartment called "Poverty Flat" and took a job as actuarial clerk in an insurance company. In a short time Ives with his partner, Julian Myrick, headed the most successful insurance agency in the country for Mutual of New York. On Wall Street, Ives's music was considered a rich man's hobby, a mild eccentricity.

When Ives married, it was to a sister of a Yale roommate and a daughter of a noted minister from Hartford who was a member of the Yale Corporation. It was a sweet coincidence that her name was Harmony Twichell. Later, unable to have children of their own, Harmony and Charles adopted a daughter, Edith.

Ives's favorite painter was Turner. He seemed untouched by the modern movement in the visual arts, and though he lived around the corner from the sensational Armory Show of 1913, there is no evidence that he saw it. Ives's attitude toward painting from nude models gives a clue not only to his tastes, but to his morals: "God never intended his handiwork to be aped by a crowd of body-flatterers. The human body has never been the inspiration for a great work of art."[5] From the library in the Redding house, it seemed that Ives leaned toward the classics. He chose song texts from many sources—Browning, Keats, Whitman, and the Concord writers. In music, Ives liked Bach and Beethoven, Brahms and Stephen

Foster. Later, he stood up vigorously for the modern movement—Ruggles, Becker, Riegger, and Cowell. But Ives never really heard their music nor did he listen to Stravinsky or Schoenberg. As for his own music, there is more of the nineteenth-century traditionalist than is generally realized. Of the almost 200 songs, for example, the most are of the nostalgic, parlor-song variety so popular in nineteenth century America.[6]

The Iveses lived in the "right" places. In New York it was a brownstone on East 74th Street where the doorknobs were polished, and a maid cooked and served the meals. Life was regular and old-fashioned. Lehman Engel, one of the young composers interested in Ives's music in the thirties and forties, described the house as Victorian and very plain. Nothing ever changed. "You knew," he said, "that the people who lived in it must be wealthy, because poor people would have decorated it with something."[7] There was a country house in Redding, Connecticut, a car, a servant. In Redding, also, little was known about Ives the composer. To all appearances, he was a successful, retired (from 1930 on due to poor health), country gentleman who liked to try his hand at farming potatoes with the help of the farmer next door. "Babe," the barber, from nearby Bethel described Ives as he came into the barber shop: "A musician? Why, old overalls, old shoes, I thought he was a gentleman farmer....I never took him for a musician!"[8]

John Kirkpatrick, noted Ives performer and scholar, is quick to point out that the Iveses were very old-fashioned. A poignant example of the conflict between old and new came when Ives's younger colleague and friend, Henry Cowell, was sent to prison on a morals charge. Ives had admired Cowell's forward thinking and experimental music ideas, but it was another matter where established morality was concerned—Ives was so shocked about Cowell's situation that he could never bring himself to discuss the matter. Kirkpatrick, when talking about the Iveses, calls them "Harmony" and "Charlie," but points out that he would never have addressed them by their given names when he knew them. This proper and somewhat old-fashioned gentleman was Charles Ives.

Ives, American Folk Hero

Charles Edward Ives was the first-born son of George Ives, bandmaster, black sheep of the Ives family who went into music instead of business and from whom his son Charles learned the rules of music. But Charlie also learned from his father about experimentation with quarter-tones, space, and other kinds of ear-stretching exercises such as playing in one key and singing in another. Charles went to church, but he also attended gospel meetings, camp meetings, ragtime performances, and parades. The *Variations on America*, written by Ives at age sixteen, have interludes so dissonant that they made the boys in the choir giggle. As for Ives at Yale, behind the proper Yalie scene, incredibly, and in total isolation, Ives was writing the music that is now considered the most innovative music by an American composer.

When Ives went into business, it was partly because he knew that he could never sell the kind of sounds he heard. Also, he had been formulating ideas about the division of art from life, and business was his way of keeping in touch with all kinds of working people and of keeping music and life as one experience, each enriching the other. Many of Ives's business ideas were innovative and experimental. He believed that the wealthy should restrict their incomes, and in line with this idea, Ives himself limited what he took from Ives and Myrick. To him the insurance business was a vehicle for protecting the helpless; he developed policies to insure children, college students, influenza victims, and widows. Within the business, Ives functioned as an educator, counseling agents and writing articles and brochures expounding his ideas and theories. It was not unusual to see a quotation from Emerson or Thoreau in a newspaper or magazine ad written by Ives. Innovative concepts, such as estate planning, first suggested by Ives, were adopted by the insurance business as a whole and have become standard usage.

Charles Ives married the prettiest girl in Hartford from the best family. Harmony had some ideas of her own; she was a trained nurse and worked in a poor section of Chicago before marrying. Harmony never told her husband to write music for recognition, approval, or social position. In fact, the young couple did not have much social life, since Ives saved nights and weekends for music-writing. A severe heart attack in 1918 curtailed Ives's activities: his composing years were virtually over, and by 1930 he retired completely from business. Ives lived on until 1954 as a semi-invalid.

It is not the biographical facts of Ives's life nor his extensive quotation of folk materials that catch the imagination of those who make of this composer a folk hero. Rather, it is Ives's unique position among "serious" composers as a man of the people that gives a clue to the reasons behind the legend. Ives was more a philosopher than a composer; he had a story to tell, a memory to relate, or a message to communicate, and music was his best medium. Ives believed that ideas could be projected in sound and that someday men might speak in one universal language of musical sounds. These ideas partially explain Ives's puzzling multiplicity of musical styles—he simply chose whatever would most vividly and directly project what he wanted to say from the multitude of musical styles and sources available. That sometimes meant layering a number of seemingly unrelated musical thoughts simultaneously, and it accounts, in large part, for the puzzling multiplicity of styles in this composer's works. To illustrate this point, let us briefly examine two Ives songs.

"Two Little Flowers" of 1921 with a text by Harmony and Charles Ives about Edith, their daughter, and her playmate Susanna is a tranquil and innocent protrait of these "two little flowers." Ives never abandoned tonality, and here, he quite naturally chose a traditional approach. There is no dissonance to disturb the peaceful garden. The poem and the song are brief and direct as though the visual image must be presented quickly before the flowers fade and the sun lowers. The voice and piano move together in a horizontal, running movement conveying the fleeting nature of ephemeral and precious youth and innocent beauty. The song, "Vote for Names, Names, Names, with Teddy, Woodrow and Bill," written for voice and three pianos or "at least three pianists," is also brief, on a single page and less than one minute in length. Each piano is assigned a different, dissonant, chordal figure to be played at regular intervals against or in tandem with the other two. About the one repeated chord Ives wrote: "Same chord hit hard over and over and over—the hot air election slogan." Another memo notes that the differences between Roosevelt, Wilson, and Taft were like "3 chords exactly alike—a hopeless chord—a chord of futility." It did not seem to matter to Ives that three pianos were needed for a one minute song. He had a political viewpoint here and chose the most forceful musical way to project it.

Ives's ideas of freedom of choices for the performer is another direction wherein he lies closer to folk music practice than to established concert rules. This flexibility, later adopted and adapted by others, has often been cited as innovative and experimental, but not so for folk artists who have always expected performances to differ one from another. There are many indications from Ives that reveal his strong desire to maintain an open-ended situation for performers. He occasionally made different written versions of certain pieces and often indicated alterations in a manuscript itself, and from musicians who had the opportunity to work with Ives, reports clearly show his reticence to pin down a definitive performance.[9] Ives's delight in the vitality of impromptu and amateur performances stems from his father and Emerson. It is an attitude of non-exclusivity. Enthusiasm and spirit were more important than polished and cultivated playing—anyone and everyone, therefore, could make music. If performer, listener, and composer could interact, Ives believed that people and nations could coexist, and if audience and performer, as well as composer, were involved in making decisions, why not people and politicians in a democratic state? This kind of impossible idealism and depth of caring are often found with folk musicians.

Before continuing this convincing case of Ives as "folk hero," it must be emphasized that we speak not of the composer's music in sound and performance, nor of his intention, but of his ideas. It would be a distortion to consider Ives's dissatisfaction with the world of concert music as an indication that he had any intention of approaching a different world. He would not have thought of himself in this context at all—not even to the extent that several other composers did—as scholar or collector.[10] Surely, one can assume that Ives might have enjoyed the word "folk" as he relished "common man" and "the masses," and he *did* often quote folk tunes, but there was nothing systematic or scholarly in his approach to folk music.

The validity of the folk hero legend increases when one considers the composer's attitudes toward commercialism, nature, ecology, privacy, and political freedom. Before Ives's music was known, he would supply scores and copies without fee or royalty to anyone interested. Later, his lawyer convinced him to take copyrights, but only with the agreement that musical earnings go toward helping new music and other composers. Even today, the estate of Charles Ives distributes substantial grants each year to help young composers, and it will continue to do so under the terms of his will. Commercialism in recording and publishing businesses infuriated Ives. He would sign a contract stating on page one that the composer make no money from the piece of music in question. The publisher would read this with high regard, turn the page to read a second condition—that likewise publisher receive no profit.

Ives, strongly influenced by Emerson and Thoreau, had an almost worshipful respect for nature and a strong sense of preservation of natural resources. Ives's song "The New River"[11] of 1912 is an outburst against pollution of the Housatonic River, long before Pete Seeger's crusade against ruination of the Hudson. Ives made himself available through his music and his literary writings, but in private life, he insisted on keeping his distance—a man's personal life and property were sacred. For heroic gesture one need not look further than Ives as an old man with beard and cane, standing in his fields among his beloved rocks and hills, shouting and waving furiously at airplanes for intruding on life and property without permission.

The use of music as a powerful weapon for political and social issues is not new with Charles Ives, but it has not been the usual domain of concert composers. Ives's political ideas were based on an unshakable belief in the goodness of the common man. He categorically refused to think that people, given their own choices, would fight and kill. His political ideas were considered naive—abolish the Electoral College and bring the vote to the people, trust the masses and not the politicians. In Ives's writings can be found a "Suggestion for a 20th Amendment" that he tried to distribute in several forms to newspapers, magazines, President, Cabinet, and Republican Convention in 1920.[12] The Amendment and articles projecting the power of people against war ("The Peoples World Nation" and "The Majority") fell on deaf ears. If his musical works with political ideas, such as "Lincoln the Great Commoner" and "The Majority," were admired, it was by the few avant-gardists, for their extraordinary musical values, and not as forces toward social betterment or political freedom. In politics and social reform, Ives was thoroughly frustrated during his lifetime, even more so than in music. The picture of this man, far ahead of his time as a composer and thinker, unrecognized and unfulfilled, bravely insisting on his own way, contributes in large part to the legend of Ives as folk hero.

The music, first and foremost, in its unique blend of nostalgia and innovation, speaks to us of our past and future; it encompasses nineteenth century America in a twentieth century voice. Charles Ives, in his music and in his life, did not choose between contradictions and paradoxes; periods and styles exist together. There is no need, therefore, to make choices. It is this combination of opposites, including Victorian gentleman and folk hero, that makes Ives a unique and extraordinary figure in American music.

[1] Vivian Perlis, *Charles Ives Remembered: An Oral History* (New Haven: Yale University Press, 1974).

[2] Theodore Timreck, "A Good Dissonance Like a Man," (1976).

[3] Ives Collection, Yale Music Library, New Haven, Connecticut.

[4] Tape Number 2A, Ives Oral History Project, Yale University.

[5] Charles E. Ives, *Charles E. Ives: Memos*, ed. John Kirkpatrick (New York: W. W. Norton Co., 1972).

[6] H. Wiley Hitchcock, *Ives* (London: Oxford University Press, 1977), 9.

[7] Perlis, *Charles Ives Remembered*, 195.

[8] Perlis, 112.

[9] Perlis, 220.

[10] For example, Henry Cowell, Ruth Crawford Seeger, Percy Grainger.

[11] Also called "The Ruined River." See *Charles E. Ives: Memos*, 162.

[12] Perlis, 78.

Myths About Black Folk Music

Dena J. Epstein

THE MISSISSIPPI-BORN WRITER Irwin Russell lived only twenty-six years, from 1853 to 1879, yet he seems to have had a better grasp of black folk music than many of the scholars who have considered themselves authorities. His poem "Christmas Night in the Quarters" pictured a celebration on a plantation including dancing to the fiddle and banjo. The stricter evangelical churches would not have approved, but these musical occasions did take place and can be verified in other contemporary sources. More than that, Russell wrote two lines that could have been taken as a motto by many of the writers who have instructed the world about black folk music:

> We form our minds by pedants' rules;
> And all we know, is from the schools.[1]

Performers and collectors of folk music take it for granted that folk music is a living, evolving body of music; that to understand it, you must first *listen* to it. But the early collectors, before the age of sound recording, were not able to recreate at will the performance itself. They had to transcribe what they heard into standard musical notation to preserve it for later study. And this act of transcription had great impact on the development of the theory that black spirituals were based on earlier white spirituals, as traditional musicologists applied to folk music the same techniques they learned to use for classical music—studying the written notes as if they were the music itself.

Many theories have grown up about black folk music in the United States, influenced by current fashions in sociology, anthropology, and history. Some of these theories have been enshrined in myths, the most influential of which were these:

Blacks arrived in the New World culturally naked.
Black spirituals were wholly derived from earlier white spirituals.
African instruments could not have been transported to the New World.
The slaves had no secular music.
The banjo was invented by white men, either in New York or Virginia.

Documentary evidence is now available to prove that each of these statements is untrue.

Myth number two, that black spirituals were wholly derived from earlier white spirituals, is no longer widely believed, but it was accepted by a whole generation of musicologists, and vestiges of it linger on in the pages of some of our most prestigious reference books. Retracing its history may be instructive in helping us to understand how intelligent, responsible scholars of an earlier day could reach conclusions that seem so wrongheaded today. The pervasiveness of this theory in musical literature is demonstrated in the 5th edition of *Grove's Dictionary of Music and Musicians* still sitting on our library shelves. The article on "Spirituals, Negro" by George Pullen Jackson, reads in part: ". . . European scholars quickly recognized the African source idea for the myth that it was. . . . A close scrutiny of the black man's collected songs and their careful comparison with those of the far earlier [i.e., white] tradition showed about half of them to be variants, either in tune or words or both, of definite songs in the white man's stock . . . " The *New Grove*, now in press, will have a new article.[2]

When I was writing *Sinful Tunes and Spirituals*,[3] I saw my purpose as the presentation of contemporary primary source material, and set aside other matters. But through the years I had been curious about the origin and growth of this theory that had always seemed dubious to me. Who were the European scholars who changed the course of American musical history, and how did they become involved?

For convenience, I used the chronology in the appendix, "The Negro-White Spiritual," to D. K. Wilgus's book *Anglo-American Folksong Scholarship Since 1898*. Wilgus, uncomfortable with the existing evidence, commented: "Early evidence is scanty and confused . . . the same evidence nourished both sides . . . .There is no trustworthy evidence before the Civil War . . ."[4] He outlined known developments, beginning with the blackface minstrel songs of the mid-nineteenth century, continuing with the emergence of the Negro spiritual during the Civil War and the tours of the various Jubilee Singers—all accepted at the time and later as supporting an African Negro origin for the spiritual. The earliest dissenting opinion he cited was that of Richard Wallaschek in his *Primitive Music* of 1893.

Wallaschek wrote before the wide use of sound recording, a pioneer in what is now called ethnomusicology. He speculated about the origins of music itself and tried to explain deviations from European traditions which he never doubted were superior. The efforts of Wallaschek and his generation were described by Mantle Hood in his book, *The Ethnomusicologist* published in 1971: "There was a great preoccupation with comparing . . . every kind of music with every other kind of music—long before the things being compared were understood. This led to the fabrication of some wondrous theories that time has proven were founded more on fancy than on fact. Altogether, it was a glorious period that stimulated the imagination and the imagination was called on rather often to fill in the unknown."[5] Wallaschek never visited

America or Africa, and never heard the music he discussed with such assurance. Statements quoted with admiration by succeeding generations of scholars read: "Speaking generally, these negro-songs are very much overrated, and . . . as a rule they are mere imitations of European compositions which the negroes have picked up and served up again with slight variations."[6] He complained that some "authorities" gave only words, neglecting to mention that some of the words were translated into German, rendering "The Yellow Rose of Texas" as "Gelbe Röslein von Indiana."[7] "Yellow Rose", of course, was a minstrel song, as were most of the others translated by Herr Busch.

For versions with music, Wallaschek relied on the transcriptions in *Slave Songs of the United States*,[8] the first published collection of these songs of 1867, and what he called "another interesting collection of Aethiopian negro melodies by Christy, *Plantation Melodies.*" Obviously he made no distinction between minstrel songs and spirituals. Although the editors of *Slave Songs* stated their transcriptions lacked the distinctive features of the music as it was performed, Wallaschek discounted this reservation, commenting: "I cannot think that these . . . deserve the praise given by the editors, for they are unmistakably 'arranged'—not to say ignorantly borrowed—from the national songs of all nations, from military signals, well-known marches, German student songs, etc."[9]

Apart from his statement about Negro spirituals, Wallaschek's book is never quoted by ethnomusicologists today, being regarded as an historic curiosity. To permit you to judge its quality for yourself, I'll quote a bit of his discussion of major and minor "keys": "It is surprising how often savages sing in the minor key. . . . African music show[s] a preference for the major key . . . and therefore we cannot say that as a rule the minor key occurs more frequently among uncivilized people as a whole; it depends upon the race or perhaps the country."[10] The full title of his book was *Primitive Music; An Inquiry into the Origin and Development of Music, Songs, Instruments, Dances and Pantomimes of Savage Races.* That he included among the "savage races" the Chinese and all peoples of the Middle and Far East is indicative of the primitive nature of his book.

He was not a stupid or an ignorant man, but he wrote when anthropology was in its infancy and ethnomusicology was still to be born as a serious discipline. In 1893 no one seemed to notice that he had not heard the music he was judging. Because he was a "European scholar" when few Americans considered themselves scholarly, he was respected and his opinions on Negro spirituals were quoted with something approaching awe. I cannot help feeling that almost anyone who had *heard* the music was better qualified to discuss it than this Viennese student of philosophy and jurisprudence.

The people who contributed to *Slave Songs of the United States* heard the music and did their best to reduce it to musical notation. Wallaschek and his successors had not heard the music, but relied on transcriptions made in standard musical notation developed for the reproduction of European music. Whatever its virtues, this system of notation could not transcribe well such qualities as polyrhythms, vibrato, tremolo, glissando, tone color, nontraditional phrasing, variations in pitch from the standard scales, including "blue notes" or the so-called "dirty tones," and the extremely common overlapping of leader and chorus in the "call and response" style. The role of improvisation was virtually ignored. It is not unfair to say that the notational system filtered out all non-European stylistic elements, retaining those common to European music. Under such circumstances, it should come as no surprise that what was transcribed resembled European music. Performance style, now regarded as supremely important, was ignored. The use of musical notation as the most reliable embodiment of the music was misapplied to folk music with distorted results. Yet until fairly recently, most discussions of Negro spirituals were based on comparing one inadequate transcription with another.

I do not maintain that the spirituals were purely African in origin. Christianity itself was an element in an acculturative process that included learning the English language and becoming accustomed to different foods, sights and sounds. A process of syncretism must have taken place—the fusion of cultures which had some common elements and many disparate ones. But the theory we are tracing maintained that white folk music was primarily or wholly the basis of the Negro spiritual.

Wilgus's chronology of the controversy listed a number of writers who based their ideas on analyses of the transcriptions, discussing scales, intervals, syncopation, and the like. Most notable was Henry Krehbiel, who published *Afro-American Folk Songs* in 1914.[11] Until the 1920s, no one conceived of another way of studying this music, and the deficiencies of the transcriptions were overlooked, most of the discussions treating them as the equivalent of the music as it was performed. Meanwhile arrangements of spirituals for concert performance grew increasingly elaborate, more like German Lieder and less like folk songs. James Weldon Johnson's *Book of American Negro Spirituals* published in 1925 is a good example.[12] A few field collectors, like Newman Ivey White[13] and Robert W. Gordon,[14] noted similarities between white and Negro songs, raising questions they could not answer.

In 1926 for the first time an authority on African music entered the controversy. Erich von Hornbostel, the head of the Phonogrammarchiv in Berlin, had heard the music in both Africa and America. A brief quotation from a review he wrote for the *International Review of Missions* has been cited as conclusive proof of a white origin for the Negro spiritual. He wrote: "American Negro songs look like European folk-songs—Scotch and English in the English-speaking areas, French and Spanish in the Creole districts."[15] Since he said they *look* like European folksongs, it was self-evident that he was discussing written versions. Indeed, the preceding sentence read: "At first sight, when comparing the written music of African and American Negroes, one would think that they have nothing at all in common." This sentence does not discuss how they *sound*, a distinction that seems to have been overlooked. Later in the same review, he further qualified his views, a passage that seems to have been completely ignored:

> Still, there is one feature in American Negro songs which is not European but African, namely the form consisting of leading lines sung by a single voice, alternating with a refrain sung by a chorus. This form, it is true, also occurs in European folksongs, but in African songs it is almost the only one used.
>
> The majority of American Negro songs, then, show a form which is comparatively scarce in European folksongs. It is improbable that the Negroes sang merely what their ancestors learned from the white people. ...The great mass of the songs now in vogue are real folksongs of American Negro origin. ...they are not mere imitations, nor are they African songs influenced by the white man, but they are songs made by the Negroes in European style.

On the next page, von Hornbostel made an even more significant statement:

> You will readily recognize an African Negro by seeing him dance and by hearing him sing. Not what he sings is so characteristic of his race, but the way he sings. This way of the Negro is identical in Africa and in America, and is totally different from the way of any other race, but it is difficult, if not impossible to describe or analyze it....
>
> In short, the American Negro songs are European in style and pattern, they are American folksongs as far as they have originated amidst American folk and culture, and they are African when sung by Negroes.[16].

Von Hornbostel's sensitivity to the performance style was derived from his firsthand experience with the music in Africa and America; he was not limited to the notated versions.

But the scholars who followed von Hornbostel lacked his firsthand knowledge. Although the phonograph was now available, it was bulky, awkward to transport, and still to be accepted in academic circles. Few scholars made use of it, continuing to rely on printed versions, thus revealing a basic insensitivity to the nature of the music. Most of their studies were in the academic tradition, textual and historical, comparing printed versions with other printed versions, as one might compare two versions of a madrigal or a motet.

A new stage in the gathering of evidence was reached when Guy Benton Johnson, of the University of North Carolina, published his *Folk Culture on St. Helena Island, South Carolina* in 1930.[17] While only one section was devoted to the

"Folk Songs of St. Helena Island," Johnson included transcriptions of songs currently sung on the island, comparing them with older published folk hymns. He exercised considerable care in analyzing the scales, melodic patterns, intervals, and modulations, but, as he paid very little attention to performance style, in effect he analyzed the transcriptions. He did not identify the transcriber nor describe the conditions under which the transcriptions were made.

Johnson was a much more careful scholar than some of his predecessors. He consulted experts on folklore, dialect, and music in the preparation of his manuscript. It is a measure of American scholarship generally at that time that no one seems to have suggested that a knowledge of African languages or musics might be helpful. Although his book represented a distinct advance over previous discussions, it was limited by a complete reliance on European material, for example, his apparent belief that a parallel between the Gullah dialect of the Sea Islands and a provincial English usage of the seventeenth century was sufficient to show a direct connection.

The strongest statement of the "white origins" school was made by George Pullen Jackson, a professor of German at Vanderbilt University, who enthusiastically explored the history of the so-called "white" spiritual. His article on Negro spirituals in *Grove's Dictionary of Music and Musicians* has already been quoted. His book *White Spirituals in the Southern Uplands* published in 1933, was exciting to read while it discussed shape-note singers. At least, it seemed so to me when I read it as an undergraduate. But even at eighteen, I *knew* something was wrong with his discussion of Negro spirituals, although I could not identify it at the time. After a history of the "white" spiritual, Jackson drew many parallels between white and Negro spirituals, some only fragments, some extended passages. Such parallels certainly did exist between nineteenth-century shape-note tunebooks and published collections of Negro songs printed later. To Professor Jackson, priority in publication was certain proof of origin. This may be accepted in copyright litigation, but it is far from true in folk music, most especially when you are dealing with a population kept illiterate by force of law. Today origin, priority, and whether the direction of influence was white-to-black, black-to-white, or in both directions are all still unestablished.

On occasion Jackson did listen to the music. He even included a chapter, "Folk Singing and Book Tunes Differ," in his 1944 book, *White and Negro Spirituals: Their Life Span and Kinship*.[19] His parallels, however, were all drawn from published versions. He seems to have regarded performance style and improvisation as relatively unimportant factors. The date of first publication was the crucial fact to him.

To summarize, the evidence cited by the "white origins" school was drawn almost entirely from notated sources, many of them arrangements for concert performance, like the *Jubilee Songs*.[20] While such reliance was unavoidable before the development of field recording equipment, the earliest collectors were well aware of the deficiencies of their transcriptions. They could not help themselves. Later discussions, however, tended to be based on the assumption that the notated versions were the equivalent of the music as it was performed, or regarded performance style as of little significance. To this extent these discussions were defective and misleading.

It is clear that analysis of the notated versions of Negro spirituals, as of other kinds of folk music, no matter how skillfully done, cannot answer questions of priority or establish lines of historic development. The writings of Jackson and other supporters of the "white origins" school prove nothing about origin or direction of influence. The parallels they present between white and Negro spirituals must be taken into consideration together with other kinds of evidence, historical, iconographic and ethnomusicological from Europe, Africa, and the Americas. But, above all, the first requirement of understanding this music is listening to it, not once, but many times, for its performance style cannot be reduced to notation. The myths that have grown up about black folk music can be dispelled by documentary proof and sensitive musical interpretation.

[1]Reprinted from the original manuscript in the Mississippi Department of Archives and History, Jackson, in *An Anthology of Mississippi Writers*, eds. Noel K. Polk and James R. Scafidel (Jackson: University Press of Mississippi, 1979), 127.

[2]*Grove's Dictionary of Music and Musicians*, 5th ed. (1954), Vol. 8. 11; *New Grove Dictionary of Music and Musicians*, 6th ed. (1980), Vol. 18, s.v. "Spirituals, Black."

[3]Dena J. Epstein, *Sinful Tunes and Spirituals: Black Folk Music to the Civil War* (Urbana: University of Illinois Press, 1977).

[4]D. K. Wilgus, *Anglo-American Folksong Scholarship Since 1898* (New Brunswick: Rutgers University Press, 1959), [345]-46.

[5]Mantle Hood, *The Ethnomusicologist* (New York: McGraw-Hill, 1971), 47.

[6]Richard Wallaschek, *Primitive Music; An Inquiry into the Origin and Development of Music, Songs, Instruments, Dances, and Pantomimes of Savage Races* (London: Longmans, Green and Co., 1893), 60. A German translation was published in 1903 with the title *Anfänge der Tonkunst.*

[7]Moritz Busch, *Wanderungen zwischen Hudson und Mississippi, 1851 und 1852* (Stuttgart: J. G. Cotta, 1854), 258-9.

[8][William Francis Allen, Charles Pickard Ware, and Lucy McKim Garrison, comps.] *Slave Songs of the United States* (New York: A. Simpson, 1867).

[9]Richard Wallaschek, *Primitive Music*, 61.

[10]Wallaschek, 145-6.

[11]Henry Edward Krehbiel, *Afro-American Folksongs: A Study in Racial and National Music* (New York: G. Schirmer, 1914).

[12]James Weldon Johnson, *The Book of American Negro Spirituals* (New York: Viking, 1925).

[13]Newman Ivey White, *American Negro Folk-songs* (Cambridge: Harvard University Press, 1928).

[14]Robert Winslow Gordon, "The Negro Spiritual," in [Society for the Preservation of Spirituals] *The Carolina Low-country* (New York: Macmillan, 1931).

[15]Erich von Hornbostel, "American Negro Songs" [review], *International Review of Missions* 15 (1926) 749.

[16]Hornbostel, 751-3.

[17]Guy Benton Johnson, *Folk Culture on St. Helena Island, South Carolina* (Chapel Hill: University of North Carolina Press, 1930).

[18]George Pullen Jackson, *White Spirituals in the Southern Uplands* (Chapel Hill: University of North Carolina Press, 1933).

[19]George Pullen Jackson, *White and Negro Spirituals: Their Life Span and Kinship* (New York: J. J. Augustin, 1944).

[20][Theodore F. Seward, comp.] *Jubilee Songs: As Sung by the Jubilee Singers of Fisk University, Nashville, Tennessee* (New York: Biglow & Main, 1872).

PART VI

Blacks and Blues

Blues and Modern Sound: Past, Present, and Future

David Evans

FROM ITS VERY BEGINNINGS as a musical form the blues has played a role in popular music and in various manifestations of the "modern sound." It has contributed to popular music at a general level as well as in specific ways to almost every major form and style of American music in the twentieth century. Yet despite these contributions, blues also remains a distinct musical form with its own traditions. Certain performers are still known specifically as "blues singers" or "bluesmen," and many of them perform virtually no other type of music. Such performers have existed throughout the history of the blues. Thus the music has had the peculiar reputation of being something both primitive and modern. Those singers and musicians who specialize in the blues are often considered crude and technically limited by others who perform different musical styles. Many artists state that they can perform blues but do not want to limit themselves to this type of music. Often they view blues as no more than raw material for development and exploitation within other musical styles and traditions.

Admittedly the blues is simple music in respect to its most basic formal characteristics. It uses brief stanza forms and generally no more than three chords in its harmonies, it often employs a pentatonic scale for the melody; and it has texts that frequently seem to skip from one topic to another with little or no logical progression or thematic or narrative unity.[1] In actuality this musical and textual simplicity or crudity is only a superficial characteristic, and blues can be shown to exhibit great subtlety of expression. But this subtlety generally stems from the innate talent of composers and performers rather than from their formal training. The apparent simplicity of the blues probably enables innate musical talent to be magnified more than in other musical forms where this talent must be harnessed to more elaborate musical and lyrical structures. Thus the blues is an ideal vehicle of expression for poor people who have little access to formal musical training. It was among such people that the blues first arose, and they have continued to pioneer the most creative developments in this music's history. Through blues music many such individuals have been able to find a vehicle of self-expression and raise themselves temporarily or even permanently out of the rut of poverty and isolation. It is the purpose of this paper to outline the contributions of blues to American music in general and to specific musical forms and traditions and to indicate the present state and possible future directions of blues both as a self-contained musical tradition and in relation to the broader spectrum of American music.

In a general sense blues could be considered to have made major contributions to American music in three areas, namely scale, form, and subject matter. In fact, each of these characteristics has been used at one time or another to define or characterize the blues. To our musical scale the blues has contributed the so-called "blue notes." These have been variously described as flatted notes, neutral pitches, waverings, sliding tones, and tonal ranges, generally at the third and seventh degrees of the scale but sometimes at other points as well. However one wants to define "blue notes," they represent a major breaking away from the European and classical scale. "Blue notes" are pervasive today throughout virtually all of American popular music as well as that of many other parts of the world. Actually these notes existed in earlier forms of Afro-American music such as spirituals and worksongs and were pointed out by some observers in the nineteenth century, but it was through blues that they spread to other American musical forms. In fact, through the 1920s the presence of "blue notes" in a song seems to have been the main criterion for calling that piece a "blues." Many songs which used ragtime or popular harmonic progressions and stanza forms were called "blues" because their scales employed "blue notes."

In respect to musical form the blues has contributed to American music the distinctive three-line AAB stanza pattern with its familiar harmonic progression. Blues has also contributed certain two-line and four-line patterns. These patterns have been elaborated in countless ways by many performers and composers, but their basic outlines are still detectable and can be found throughout popular music. Another important formal characteristic of blues is the role that the instrument or instruments play in respect to the singing, namely that of responding to and interacting with the vocal line. Instruments in the blues do not merely have an accompaniment function but rather represent additional voices. Their lines are integral parts of the song itself. This elevated role for instruments within vocal music has now become a standard feature of American popular music, one that is due to the influence of the blues. These formal characteristics of verse and harmonic pattern and instrumental role are the ones that most scholars have used to define the blues.

Blues singers themselves generally define the blues as a feeling or an attitude toward life. Basically blues songs avoid sentimentality and the idea of progress toward some ideal state of things. Instead they dramatize and celebrate the ups and downs of life, enabling singers and their audiences to externalize some of their strongest feelings, particularly those dealing with interpersonal relationships between the sexes. Blues contains a realism and an earthiness that were generally lacking in earlier types of folk and popular song but which have gradually become more prevalent in this century in all types of songs.

Blues originated as a distinct type of music shortly before the beginning of the twentieth century.[2] This was a time of major new developments in many areas of black music. A new generation had just reached maturity, born and raised outside the confines of slavery. This generation broke with the music of the past and created new forms such as blues, jazz, ragtime, vocal quartet music, folk ballads, and the new music of the Pentecostal churches featuring the use of a variety of instruments. Out of all of these musical forms blues probably represented best the music of the lowest class of black society, the poorest people in the rural areas of the Deep South, landless sharecroppers and tenant farmers, hoboes and migratory common laborers, and those who streamed into the urban slums of the South and the North seeking relief from oppressive rural social and economic conditions. Blues was therefore the most "underground" and most "folk" of these new musical forms and consequently one of the last to be popularized. In fact, it still retains a strong folk and underground component with many traditional musical and lyrical elements and many regional, local, and individual stylistic manifestations.

This status can be seen clearly in the reactions of a number of individuals to blues music at the time of its earliest development. Lucius Smith, a ninety-four-year-old banjo player living in Sardis, Mississippi, was already performing string band music for square dancing when blues came on the scene. He didn't like the new music because it was "out of order" and caused people to dance "at random." He associated it with drinking and rowdiness.[3] W. C. Handy, who is often called the "Father of the Blues," actually considered the folk blues to be raw material for popular songs. Handy was a trained musician and could not have composed within a folk blues style, though he had the foresight to recognize good material and incorporate it into his many fine formal compositions. His statements and writings indicate that he was very much aware of the differences between the folk and formal products.[4] J. Mayo Williams, a college educated black man who was a pioneer in the blues recording industry, advertised Blind Lemon Jefferson, the first major folk blues singer to record, in 1926 as "a real old-fashioned blues singer," who sang "old-time tunes" and played guitar "in a real southern style."[5] Many white writers in the late teens and 1920s emphasized the blues' alleged "underworld" associations and unsavory aspects of the songs' subject matter.[6] A similar reaction took place among some whites in the 1950s, when blues once again had significant impact on white popular consciousness. Then the blues was characterized as "jungle music" and its so-called "primitive" aspects pointed out, accompanied by dire warnings about the consequences for white youths who listened or danced to this music.

During its early years blues influenced other emerging popular musical forms. Blues rhythms entered ragtime music, and to some extent the earliest blues compositions on sheet music were simply considered a variety of ragtime music. The blues form and blue notes, however, were foreign to the spirit of ragtime and never were very well incorporated into that musical form. Blues was probably even more at home in early jazz music, as witnessed by the fact that many of the first jazz recording groups featured blues heavily in their repertoires. Blues was also prominent in the repertoires of early vocal quartets like the Norfolk Jazz Quartet and the Birmingham Quartet who began recording in the 1920s. Though blues appeared less in jazz and vocal group music of the 1930s, it made a comeback in bebop music of the 1940s. A large number of the classic bebop pieces of artists like Charlie Parker are actually in the blues form although the harmonies have been greatly altered. Modern jazz has continued to make heavy use of the blues form. The blues also made a strong comeback with vocal groups in the 1950s, although its popularity has since declined in this form of music. Blues has had an important influence on gospel music as well. Thomas A. Dorsey, who is generally considered the father of black gospel music, was a former blues singer, musician, and composer before he entered the gospel field. Blues also seems to have influenced the styles of a number of important pioneer gospel performers such as Blind Willie Johnson, Sister Rosetta Tharpe, and the Staples Singers.

Blues not only influenced other forms of black music, but it has also had a great impact on white music. In fact, it has even influenced the music of some minority ethnic groups in America. Hawaiian music, for example, has incorporated a great number of blues into its repertoire since the 1920s, and there has developed a complex interrelationship between Hawaiian guitar playing and blues slide guitar style. The music of the French-speaking Cajuns of Louisiana has also been heavily influenced by blues in the last few decades, even though the main instruments of accordion and fiddle are unorthodox in black blues tradition.

During the 1920s blues exerted some influence on classical music as seen in the work of composers like George Gershwin. Blues was also very prominent in popular white vaudeville music during this same period. There are many recordings available from the late teens and 1920s of blues by vaudeville artists like Al Bernard, George O'Connor, Cliff Edwards, Marie Cahill, Sophie Tucker, Margaret Young, Dolly Kay, and Marion Harris. The singing was usually rather stiff compared to the work of contemporary black recording artists, but the important thing is that the attempt was being made.

Perhaps the most notable impact of blues on white music has been in the area of country and western music. The man who is often considered to be the first real star of commercial country music, Jimmie Rodgers, rose to fame on the basis of his blue yodels, basically folk blues with yodeling at the ends of some lines and on refrains. Rodgers's popularity resulted in a host of imitators and followers, some of whom are still active in country music. Later on in the 1930s western swing music became quite popular as exemplified by the work of artists like Bob Wills, Milton Brown, and W. Lee O'Daniel, all of whom featured with their bands many blues taken from popular records by black artists. In the 1940s and 1950s the honky tonk style, as exemplified by Hank Williams, utilized many blues tunes. Countless country music stars claim to have been influenced in their formative musical years by black blues performers, and often this influence was direct rather then through records or radio. In the last couple of decades blues seems to have played less of a role in country music, but several recent blues song hits may be indications of a comeback for the blues.

Rock and roll music grew out of a mixing of blues and country music that first took place in the 1950s. This is seen most dramatically in the early work of Elvis Presley and some of his contemporaries who recorded for the Sun Record Company of Memphis. Each of Presley's earliest records contained a blues on one side backed by a country tune. The blues songs were Presley's adaptations of pieces that had recently been popularized by black recording artists. Jerry Lee Lewis, Carl Perkins, Bill Haley, and other early white rock and roll stars also recorded a very high percentage of blues. Their black rock and roll counterparts like Chuck Berry, Fats Domino, Little Richard, and Bo Diddley also recorded a great many blues, while some even more traditional artists like Big Joe Turner and Jimmy Reed had major hits with straight blues pieces. By the early 1960s the role of blues had declined within rock and roll music due to changing popular tastes and a reactionary stance of certain forces within the music industry who found blues to be too earthy. At this time white appreciation for blues shifted to folk music revival circles. Though the folk revival was a somewhat underground movement that produced few popular hits, and hardly any of these being blues, it did expose millions of young whites, including many musicians, to the music of highly traditional folk blues singers like Lightnin' Hopkins, John Lee Hooker, Muddy Waters, Mississippi John Hurt, Big Joe Williams, Son House, and Brownie McGhee and Sonny Terry. Many performers who later enjoyed successful careers in popular music, such as Bob Dylan, came out of the folk revival movement of the early and mid-1960s. Big Joe Williams, in fact, to this day claims to have discovered Bob Dylan, and it is true that some of Dylan's first commercial recordings were as a harmonica player on some Williams tracks that appeared on an album on the Spivey label. By the late 1960s several white artists from folk revival backgrounds had formed amplified blues bands, and one group, Canned Heat, even had several big hits with blues tunes. Meanwhile, British groups like the Beatles, Rolling Stones, and Yardbirds had been copying the earlier records of Chuck Berry, Howlin' Wolf, Slim Harpo, Muddy Waters, and other black stars and making a major impact on young white American audiences. During the 1970s the blues influence on rock and roll became less direct, although blues-influenced lead guitar playing became the norm. Today most rock groups perform a few blues, though few maintain mass popularity by doing mainly or exclusively blues. Nevertheless, millions of whites are now familiar with blues and enjoy it when they hear it though they may prefer it in limited doses or in diluted form.

Blues has had a continuous history of stylistic development among blacks throughout this century in addition to influencing so many other forms of music. In general, this development has moved in the direction of greater musical sophistication and complexity. There has, however, always been a folk blues tradition. Folk blues achieved considerable popularity among blacks through phonograph records in the late 1920s, and while this popularity declined somewhat in the 1930s, the folk styles by no means disappeared. In fact, they made a strong comeback on records and in clubs in the late 1940s and the 1950s. But by the end of the 1950s blues had begun to decline seriously in popularity among blacks.

This slump lasted through the 1970s. Blues received less and less jukebox and radio play. Record companies began dropping blues artists or else orienting their releases toward the growing white audience for blues. New and younger blues artists were not recorded and promoted, and the black audience for blues began growing increasingly older and smaller. The top blues singers of 1980, such as B. B. King, Albert King, Little Milton, Bobby Bland, Muddy Waters, and John Lee Hooker are the same ones who were stars in 1960. I think the reason for this decline in popularity is that blues seemed to many blacks to be inconsistent with the aims of the Civil Rights movement. Blues seemed to represent old attitudes and living conditions rather than progress. It was unsophisticated music and had associations with the Old South and with an older generation that had learned to live with segregation. A musical generation gap developed among blacks from the late 1950s through the 1970s, just as a gap also developed among whites. But whereas many young whites embraced the blues as their symbol of rebellion, blacks by and large rejected this same music and turned instead to the soul sounds of James Brown, Wilson Pickett, Aretha Franklin, and the Supremes. These artists seemed to capture in their music the spirit of what younger blacks were striving for. Today the blues is definitely a minority musical taste among blacks.[7]

What, then is the future of the blues? Is it destined to fade away and eventually die out as the older artists leave the scene? Will the music be sustained, as some have predicted, only by white musicians? I think not. Instead I detect a serious renewal of interest in blues among young black people. At present this is still largely an underground movement, but within two or three years I predict it will make a major impact on black popular music. Just as a new generation born outside of slavery created the blues, so now a new generation has come to maturity that grew up in the Civil Rights era. Not all of the Civil Rights battles have been won by any means, but the gains that have been made have allowed many people to look back on their historical and cultural past and reassess it. A realization is occurring that the generations who had to live with slavery and segregation did not simply passively accept it but rather remained able to create significant expressions of the human spirit such as the spirituals and the blues. Undoubtedly the recent popular television series and book, *Roots*, by Alex Haley has had much to do with this reassessment of the past. But I think *Roots* simply captured the spirit of a movement that was bound to take place at this time. In fact, a "roots" phenomenon has also been apparent in recent years among young whites, stimulated in part by the recent American Bicentennial. Young members of regional and ethnic groups everywhere are seeking identity in their "roots" and attempting to restore their ties with the past that had been broken during the "generation gap" of the last twenty or more years. Black people too are increasingly looking upon themselves as members of an ethnic group with a distinctive history and cultural tradition, just like other American ethnic groups, and not simply as black Americans who have less of everything that other Americans have because of past and present injustices.

This "roots" phenomenon has manifested itself in the blues in a number of ways that I have been able to observe. Older blues musicians, who ten years ago used to drive young people away in disgust with their music, now report that youngsters are flocking around them trying to learn blues or wanting to form bands with them. Many older and middle aged bluesmen are now starting to train their children in this music and form family bands, now that the "roots" emphasis has made the family tradition something to be highly valued. Outdoor folk festivals, concerts, and television specials on blues have demonstrated to young blacks that there is widespread, even international interest in this music and that there are opportunities for significant monetary income and fame in the blues.

Several examples from the Mid-South should illustrate my point. Jessie Mae Hemphill, a middle aged but still youthful singer and guitarist from Como, Mississippi, has gone back to blues after more or less giving it up for about twenty years. She plays an early model electric guitar that was formerly owned by her late aunt and has reverted to her maiden name of Hemphill in order to emphasize the family tradition of musicianship. She is the fourth generation of musicians in the Hemphill family and is very concerned to carry on the family association with music. Her compositions deal with her life today, but the musical style is consciously archaic. She looks to a career in music as a way to escape the cycle of rural poverty and jobs cleaning house for rich white people. So far several major festival appearances, a tour, a spot on a Memphis television news program, and a record have generated considerable local interest in her music as well as doubled her yearly income.

The Fieldstones are a young five-piece blues band that plays every weekend at a lounge in Memphis in a hard postwar blues style. The members of the group are in their thirties and forties. Lois Brown, the bass player and their main spokesperson, says that at one time the band was not certain of its musical direction but they got together and decided that blues was the kind of music they really wanted to play and they have stuck with it ever since. They are now packing in large crowds, almost entirely black and covering a full range of ages with the average age probably being about the same as that of the band members. Leroy Martin, who was sitting in with the band recently and who is also in his thirties, told me that he really loves the blues and gave me a long history of the development of his guitar playing starting with a piece of broom wire on the side of a wall when he was a boy. Jimmy Holmes is a thirty-two-year-old graduate of Jackson State University, who decided not to pursue a career in teaching but instead returned to his home town of Bentonia, Mississippi, where he operates the Blue Front Cafe. He learned some blues as a boy from Henry Stuckey, the same man who taught the great Skip James about fifty years earlier, but Holmes gave it up in his high school and college years. In the last year, however, he has been following another older local musician, Jack Owens. Holmes plays occasionally at his cafe and encourages other blues musicians of all ages to play there also. He also has begun holding a two-day "festival" with barbecue and blues music on his forty-acre farm north of town on Fourth of July weekend. He says last year 400 people turned out, and he expects many more this year. Holmes states that blues to him is an important part of the black heritage and should not be allowed to die out.

R. L. Burnside is a fifty-three-year-old blues musician from Independence, Mississippi, who has a family band with his sons and son-in-law, all in their late teens and early twenties. Their music ranges from archaic folk blues to relatively modern blues with something of a disco beat. A younger thirteen-year-old son shows even more traditional tastes in blues music than do his older brothers. Many other youngsters in their teens and twenties, including a number of local whites, come to Burnside's house to listen to the music and dance. Quite a few of them are beginning musicians themselves. The youngsters are adamant that blues is their favorite type of music. One of the most dramatic examples of the "roots" phenomenon is Andrew Turner, a twenty-three-year-old second cousin of the famous Ike Turner from Clarksdale, Mississippi. Andrew has been learning blues from older local musicians and playing both acoustic and electric guitar. He has been going to the recently opened Delta Blues Museum in the public library in Clarksdale and checking out records and videotapes of blues in all styles. He even obtained a tablature book of Delta blues styles and has been trying to learn some of the songs of Mississippi John Hurt, one of the first generation of blues guitarists. Turner played on a record by Raymond Hill, and he is talking of eventually forming a band of his own and trying to make something of his music. Young blacks are increasingly attending blues concerts and festivals, such as the Beale Street Festival in Memphis and the Delta Blues Festival in Greenville, Mississippi. In fact the audiences at these festivals last year were predominantly black with all ages well represented. Interestingly enough, the most country or "folk" blues styles and the older performers got just as good a response and sometimes better than the slicker, more modern performers. Big Joe Williams and R. L. Burnside were smash hits at Greenville, as were country artists Ranie Burnette, Jessie Mae Hemphill, and Napoleon Strickland in Memphis.

I predict that this roots emphasis will intensify in the next few years with increasing media exposure, festivals, and presentation in the schools. The younger blues players are still mainly working as instrumentalists and generally seem to be a bit shy about singing blues. Perhaps they feel unready to try to match the power of the older singers. But I don't expect it to take long to overcome this hurdle. All the music needs at this point is for one or two attractive and good young performers to get the right media exposure with a good selling record or a major television appearance. This is bound to happen soon, and when it does, I think we will see hundreds of other young blues singers and musicians appearing out of nowhere and trying to get in on the action. I believe that whites will continue to participate in blues but will by no means take the music over. Whites will continue to come to blues from folk revival, rock, and country music backgrounds, but rather than borrow a little from blues and then go off and create some new synthetic style, I believe whites will increasingly participate in blues on black musical terms. In fact, I have noticed that many of the blues bands in Mississippi have one or two white members, and I understand that this has been the case in Chicago for several years. These would appear to be white musicians who have more than a superficial commitment to the blues.

I see the blues finally attaining a status that it has always had but which has not been fully recognized by most Americans, namely that of a distinctive stream within American music with a history and stylistic development of its own as well as an enormous influence on other musical forms in this country and throughout the world. I see a growing parity in this country between folk, popular, and classical styles of music, which will benefit blues in achieving the stature it deserves. I also see an increasing appreciation for innate talent and artistry to the point where they are valued equally with formally developed technical skills. Musicians and their audiences will go beyond the apparent simplicity of the blues form to appreciate the subtleties of expression that can result from innate abilities. The fruits of this new consciousness should be apparent within a few years in a renewed status and popularity for blues music in all segments of American society.

[1] A more detailed discussion of the formal characteristics of the blues is presented in David Evans, *Big Road Blues: Tradition and Creativity in the Folk Blues* (Berkeley: University of California Press, 1982), 16-32.

[2] The origins and early development of blues are discussed in greater detail in Evans, 32-59.

[3] Lucius Smith died in 1980 about a month after this paper was delivered. His statement on blues is printed at length in Evans, 47-48.

[4] W. C. Handy, *Father of the Blues* (New York: Collier, 1970), 75-92.

[5] Samuel Charters, *The Bluesmen* (New York: Oak, 1967), 177, 180.

[6] See, for example, "Enigmatic Folksongs of the Southern Underworld," *Current Opinion*, 67 (July-December, 1919), 165-66; Newman I. White, *American Negro Folk-Songs* (Cambridge, Mass.: Harvard University Press, 1928), 389; Guy B. Johnson, "Double Meaning in the Popular Negro Blues," *Journal of Abnormal and Social Psychology*, 22 (1927-28), 12-20.

[7] For an elaboration of this view see Michael Haralambos, *Right On: From Blues to Soul in Black America* (London: Eddison, 1974).

[8] Several of these younger artists can be heard on High Water Records (c/o David Evans, Music Department, Memphis State University, Memphis, TN 38152). Andrew Turner is heard on Raymond Hill, "Going Down"/Lillie Hill, "Cotton Fields - Boss Man," High Water 408. Jessie Mae Hemphill is heard on "Jessie's Boogie"/"Standing in My Doorway Crying," High Water 409. R. L. Burnside and his band are heard on "Bad Luck City"/"Jumper Hanging Out on the Line," High Water 410. The Fieldstones are heard on "Looking for a Fox"/"Blues at Nighfall," High Water 412, and "Please Don't Put Me Outdoors"/"The Thing," High Water 413. High Water has also produced albums by Hemphill and Burnside for Vogue Records of France.

Black Music: Its Roots, Its Popularity, Its Commercial Prostitution

Amiri Baraka

MOST PEOPLE, by now, except for the very young, the willfully or conditionally ignorant, or racists, know the origins of two important American musics, blues and jazz. They are, historically and originally black musics, or part of Afro-American musical tradition. They are also, and fewer might understand this, the major framework in which the majority of popular and "serious" American music has emerged. (I make the distinction popular *and* serious only to take into consideration the narrowmindedness of academics, bathed as they are in such essentially elitist false distinctions!)

The roots of black music are, of course, the African people and their tradition, especially as they came to be reshaped by the slave trade and American slavery. And as these peoples and their various national traditions (because they came to America as various nationalities, what you call tribes), came to exist in the New World, especially the United States, where finally these many groups came to be transformed into one new nationality, the African-American, by the nineteenth century.

Blues carries with it Africa and Afro-America, shaped in a land of white domination. It carries slavery and degradation, and both the memory of Africa, and the reality of the African-American developing a further variation of African culture, like Afro-American life itself, is an amalgam of African as well as European (English, Spanish, French) and Native American elements. America itself is this as well. But as Bruce Franklin, author of *The Victim as Criminal and Artist*, said in a recent *Minnesota Review*, "The most distinctive feature of United States history is Afro-American slavery and its consequences. This truth is at the heart of our political, economic and social experience as a nation-state. It is also at the heart of our *cultural* experience, and therefore the slave narrative," (for instance) "is not peripheral but central to American culture."[1]

The centrality of the black experience to shaping American culture is not understood, like when chocolate syrup is dropped into milk, it does undergo some serious change, but look at the milk! What is represented as "official" American culture by the rulers and their messengers is one thing, but the actuality of American culture is quite another. So that American literature in its official university version is mainly writing by a few white men, but to speak in reality of American literature means that it must "include the literature of several peoples, including the Afro-American nation," to quote Franklin again.

I know I shock no one by saying that it is normal ruling class procedure to portray American culture as suffocatingly white, but it is also not completely unusual to find even Afro-American culture depicted as crude black versions of something Euro-Americans do with a great deal more significance and profundity!

People who will tell you that they are normally intelligent seem put upon or embarrassed or at a loss to talk about blues and jazz as they fundamentally exist, i. e., as vectors of Afro-American culture. The fact that there are white blues and whites playing jazz simply demonstrates the strength of the music, and what should be meant by the term American culture. But there is nothing strange about the chief practitioners of this music being black. Just as no one is made uptight by the fact that most practitioners, or at least the chief practitioners, of European concert music are Europeans (except perhaps officials of Civil Rights organizations sponsored by Standard Oil and Carnegie).

In *Blues People*[2] I tried to express a fundamental perception of mine and many other people that the music changes when the people change—it develops as the people develop, and reflects that development and the twists and turns of those lives that create it. Black music moves from African to African with some foreign elements (English, Spanish, French, Native American), becomes work songs, becomes more "Americanized." It becomes Afro-Christian, at one point, and develops spirituals. And the secular, the nonreligious develops as well, sung tales, poems, the hollers, shouts, arhoolies that are the parents and later form of developed blues. The blues is a simple verse form put to music, the music simple, reflecting the level of productive forces of the slave and ex-slave society, a lone man accompanying himself on guitar or harmonica, or with his own grunts and whistles. Verse put to music, but verse begins *with* music and dancing as a special form of human activity. The form blues took was the ancient demarcation of the elimination of dance (as working in the fields is a form of dance, and is how the first dances in the world came into being) so that we have the versifier, the magician, in motion through the South. Rural, a farmer or ex-farmer, but also a secular person in the main, disconnected, at least, with the Christian rituals to a certain extent. But the religious and the secular always feed each other.

Slavery enforced a "stability" that ceased to exist in the same measure after the Civil War. So, afterwards, the blues singer was in many cases a migratory person, a wanderer. But the blues matrix was rooted in the Southern black experience. The Civil War is important to any discussion of black culture and art, since it is the transitional instrument in American history, and the importance and particularity of black relationship to the Civil War and the Reconstruction which followed should be fairly clear.

For one thing, the Civil War was supposed to mean an integration of black people democratically into the United States. This was the belief of the slaves, and a great many others, but apparently never of the rulers. The Reconstruction governments which the Freedmen's Bureau supposedly set up to help in the transfer of land and to ensure the rights of the slaves, seemed to indicate that blacks would be soon Americans, freed from the oppression of slavery. The passage of the Thirteenth, Fourteenth, and Fifteenth Amendments also gave the impression that a genuine black suffrage was at hand. But by the 1870s little land had actually changed hands, and that that had was being contested or roughed off away from the ex-slaves. The concept of 40 acres and a mule, which would seem to be a fundamental minimum for the slave to receive after two centuries of slavery, simply did not happen. And any brief attention to the history of Europe will show that in the various antifeudal democratic struggles, whether in England, Germany, France or Russia, the freed peasants received a settlement in land as the basis for the supposed existence of a post-feudal democracy. Not so for blacks in the United States.

In 1876, once the industrialists and bankers headquartered on Wall Street had stripped the Southern slavocrat landowners of most of their political and economic power, and reduced them to agents of these powerful Northern capitalists, the black motion toward democracy was sold out. The infamous Hayes-Tilden Compromise returned the Southern states to the slavocrat's hands to manage for Wall Street, and the Klan was permitted to drive black people back into virtual slavery.

This was the end of any chance of integrating black people into the social and political fabric of America based on democracy. The Black Codes, Jim Crow laws, segregation and discrimination that were now made into law, the antidemocratic practices that were now legalized, made the possibility of blacks melting in the American melting pot impossible. So even though the milk is changed, and is not white, but tan, so there is also a big unassimilable lump of chocolate at the very bottom of the mixture, unintegrated, exploited, oppressed for whom democracy is either meaningless, or means self-determination! For the post-Reconstruction social restrictions completely isolated blacks, particularly in the South, from entrance into democratic America, so that in the Black Belt South all the conditions combined to see to the emergence of an oppressed Afro-American nation, where before there were ex-slaves supposed to be integrated into multinational America!

This is the basis, even today, for the essential separation of the black masses, not only in the black South, but even in the twenty-odd cities we live in outside of the South, which are simply ghetto reproductions of the Black Belt. It is a continuing guarantor of the contrasting existence of an Afro-American culture, inside and yet outside of American culture. So that, when we speak of black music, we are speaking of the music of another nation, one that exists inside the American nation-state. A nation whose liberation can only come by revolutionary means. A nation whose liberation will mean self-determination, the right of the black masses to decide what their relationship will be with any America, even a socialist America. Black control of their own political and economic realities. So that, in essence, the Black Liberation Movement is a struggle for land and power—self-determination. Political control by the black masses of the entire lower South.

Black culture, like black people, and black art, is a separate entity, yet is easily exploitable by the ruling class of the oppressor nation, with much less flourish than a colonial relationship, since the black nation exists within the borders of the continental United States. The Afro-American nation in the black South and black people throughout the United States suffer from national oppression, a system of exploitation and robbery, forcible restriction of rights. This oppression is maintained by the big white landowners, the multinational corporations, all sanctioned and protected by the United States imperialist state. But what is more, there are sections of the white middle class and even an upper stratum of white workers who share the spoils of that robbery!

It is important that we understand these sociopolitical and economic facts if we are to understand the roots, popularity, and characteristic commercial exploitation of the music. The ex-slaves, after the war, could carry their constantly evolving music away from the plantation, and its absolute control, and this fact itself was further influence upon the music.

New Orleans was important to the early development of urban blues and jazz because it represented the higher synthesis of divergent cultures a city can make. New Orleans had the French, Spanish, English, African, and Native American streams of life flowing together in many ways. Coming into such cities, black music, the sung verse form, and the body of music and musical forms that developed with it had to reflect this. Its form and content would come more and more to reflect city life. The urban experience has been a key transformer of black life and the culture and art that issue from it.

The Afro-American culture that had come to develop by the nineteenth century had developed a *national* element to the matrix of its definition. That culture expressed itself however it had to, as all cultures do. So that coming into the city, given the form and example of the European marching bands and orchestras, of European instruments (no matter what these sounded like to the black ear) could only propose another kind of Afro-American music, urban blues and jazz.

Urban blues, and certainly jazz, are more accessible to Americans in General (a small town outside Mediocre, Ohio?). They are more accessible because postslavery black people are more accessible to Americans in general, rather than just their masters on the plantations. There is more mobility to blacks, plus the fact that now the experience they sang and played about was literally a broader one. So the people, the experience (content), and the music (form) are more available by the end of the nineteenth century.

Black music goes up the river because the people do. "Goin' to Chicago" is literally the story of great numbers of blacks headed out of the Black Belt, with some jumping off in Memphis and Kansas City, or striking out deeper in the Territories and Texas, even headed straight out west to Disneyland. But in the beginning the great majority were headed straight up the river, as far as they could get from the scene of the crime, and this meant Chicago and then New York. The magnet was the promise of jobs offered by the Northern industrialists as America made ready for its debut as an imperialist state, or full fledged imperialist state. The Mexican ripoff was a rehearsal; the Cuban, Puerto Rican, Phillipine ripoff was the full up appearance. All in motion to World War I, and the full credentialization as a world imperialist power. Blacks were also fleeing a boll weevil epidemic, the Klan fascism of the South, and the music was carried with them as they booked.

Black arrival in the North, to those Northern cities, in the total conditions of the end of the nineteenth century and the beginning of the twentieth had an effect internationally. The Harlem Renaissance that is identified with Afro-American literature and other arts emerges at this time, by the twenties. Langston Hughes and Claude McKay are the most impressive personalities of this period, as poets, novelists, and intellectuals, but there were many more. And the Renaissance itself, which was not at all limited to literature, signified the appearance of an urban black intelligentsia, and the fact that the largely peasant black masses were now undergoing a transformation from small farmers to industrial workers, from rural Southerners to urban Northerners (even though 52 percent of the entire black population still lives in the Black Belt even today).

It is in this environment that black music reaches a new maturity and power. The big bands represent the culmination at one point of the Afro-American cultural impulse totally conversant with Euro-American technical facility and theory. The result, of course, is Duke Ellington. Duke's synthesis of the slave memory, the peasant struggle and desire, and the newly assumed urban persona are classic. Black music is kept from its fullest classic statement by the limitation of productive forces under national oppression and monopoly capitalism. Bartok's use of Gipsy elements in synthesis to provoke a widening of basic intellectual perception is what is wanted. Duke could come closest to this, because he struggled to keep a large orchestra together, no matter what, because he understood that that could be the most expanded expression of the basic Afro-American musical impulse.

The twenties are called the Jazz Age, because that is when the music comes more fully into the consciousness of the entire society. And even harnessed to the ridiculous racism of a segregated Cotton Club where he had to play "jungle music," Ellington's music described America in a way and from a point of view, with a sensibility, it could feel was much deeper than the shallow fakery of Tin Pan Alley. Black life was and is to a great extent a shadow, a darkness, an invisibility for the white majority, but it is literally the blood flowing in America's veins, since rhythm is the beat of life, the heart itself, sending food to the whole body. Without rhythm the body dies. African music was always more rhythmically complex than European music, the complexity of which was largely harmonic. Ellington could take the harmonies, hook them up with the dynamic African heartbeat and create melodies that were the path of the new black adventurers in the cities, in the still to-be-defined twentieth century. (So the South is the *heartland* of America, because that's where the beat comes from, and its reproductions in the other twenty cities.)

Though the music has constantly changed in reflection of the people themselves, in their twists and turns and facing their ever new challenges, it reflects not only black people themselves but their version of America. It is a deeper America, a more complex America, because blacks survive only because of their knowledge of white America (to paraphrase Jimmy Baldwin). Black music looks at America from the outside, as an American expression that cannot be totally assimilated because its creators are denied total access to America. The slave master's version of America could not be true, otherwise he would have to denounce himself at every turn, accuse and demean himself, beat and curse himself like a classical madman. The slave master cannot tell about the life in America as harsh and as real as it really is. First he has not experienced its total harsh reality. He is in the drawing room, the rest of the world is known only to the servants. But he tells us what life is at the top, so the slave knows. And the slave also knows from grim reality what life is at the bottom.

Black music is an American music expanded past the experience of the average American. Because it is, at the same time, a foreign music. It is popular with blacks because it literally is them; it is popular (its basic impulse, even if watered down, or merely translated by Anglo-American players) among whites, to the extent that it is, because it is a people's music. It gets down. It is about the life of the downed, yet its dignity is in its fantastic sophistication even at the moment of would-be, should-be humiliation and actual despair.

But the music and culture of the white workers and farmers, the white majority in this country, is not to be found regularly in the Kennedy or Lincoln Centers or the universities, either. The relationship of most white people to the American system is that they are exploited workers, but they do not suffer national oppression or racism, and they have been melted culturally into a melting pot. And their enemies are the same enemies as the Afro-American peoples, the 6/10ths of 1 percent of the population that own the means of producing wealth in this country, the monopoly capitalist class.

The music that white workers listen to is much closer in

many ways to black music than to the official culture of the bourgeois ruling class in this country. Country and western music, rock and their many variations are much closer to blues and Afro-American music than the European music mashed on us as high culture by the Establishment. For one thing, in my view, whites in the Black Belt South, constitute a national minority whose culture is more directly influenced by the Afro-American people than anyone else in the society.

Ask the rulers or their intellectuals what is the *serious* music of the United States and they will be at a loss for words. When you first ask them about great music, they will try to take you to Europe, but once you say, hey, come out of Europe, what about over here in America, they might mumble Aaron Copland, or Gershwin, the more astute will tell you Charles Ives, but that is national oppression and racism you're hearing, and a light taste of eighteenth-century European colonialism. I mean, they cannot say Duke Ellington, the Hot Five, Charlie Parker, John Coltrane, Bessie Smith, Billie Holiday. It is to be *unreal*.

American culture is called "pop" so that it is removed from consideration as "serious." But then the rulers still push a little eighteenth-century British colonialism, even though George Washington and them won that first anticolonial war. They talk about English Departments and this *ain't* even England! American Studies and programs to study American folk culture are still basically outlaws. Black and other oppressed nationality studies came about in the sixties only because of the rebellions. The first Black Studies program happened in 1967 in San Francisco, the same spring the Black Panthers, many of whom went to San Francisco State where Black Studies was born, went up into the Sacramento legislature with their weapons. Nineteen sixty-seven was also the year blacks got their first United States Senator since the destruction of the Reconstruction—but that's the year Detroit and Newark went up in smoke.

American Studies to academics is still a bandit; black culture is even further assaulted by the existence of national oppression and racism. Black culture exists in the same fashion as black people in this society, class exploited and nationally oppressed. Black music brings a dimension to American life that is used like coal in a furnace, but it is literally ripped off. When you want to conjure up what America was like in the twenties, some Fletcher Henderson will do it. In fact, hey, don't all the backgrounds of those films made then sound like ...? But then listen to your common TV detective story with the musical score muffled and it is a totally different thing you're watching. A whole sophistication and dynamism is removed without the black music in the background. But the music is literally taken and used and the majority of its creators are misused in the same fashion as black people in general. Not only the "covers" who do black tunes for white delectation, but the sidemen with famous black musicians who wind up as musical directors for TV stations, or winning Academy Awards in Hollywood, while their old buddy and mentor is still doing one night stands. Or maybe it's the Captain and Tenille who can patch one blood sounding song together and coax fame and fortune and a TV series out of it, or the body snatchers like the Osmonds who become media stars based on sucking the blood of the Jacksons. But it is really not even that, it is simply that as long as the national oppression of the black masses exists there will be, minimally, resentment, because all cultures, world wide and historically, have learned from each other and exchanged categories of perception, but this can be positive only based on equality. In the current social degeneracy, blacks, at the bottom of society, can in the main only give up the energy, the ideas, the concept, the blood, the "raw material," while Whitman or Goodman, Mangione or Rod Stewart get over, bullshitting that they, like the old and new line imperialists, have got the finished product.

So black music is viewed as raw material to be wrung dry of what it is for you know who. The black innovator or innovation is "covered" and swallowed. The mind bandits who manipulate the media for the rulers can create a dozen android clones to replace any black anything, and pretend that black thing never existed. Usually, by denying the black innovator material resources or intellectual satisfaction, they can ensure that he won't exist long.

Just as in the forties, the big record companies manufactured hundreds of big "swing" bands in imitation of Henderson, Ellington, Lunceford, Basie, and the others. The mind bandits created a monopoly music, and several traveling bands for each one of its white swing stars, so they could be in several different places at the same time, raking in the cash, playing deadly imitations of the big swinging black bands. Swing went quickly from verb to noun.

But for blacks the big band music wasn't supposed to sound like that, like dollars rotting, and once it did, they went off and did something else, like broke into small experimenting groups and created bebop. When the monopolists began to mass produce commercial cool in the fifties as an antidote to real bebop, which had just restored the complex rhythms and blues of the Afro-American to the music, and the legitimate cool of the Pres to Miles and Miles-Mulligan sides were replaced by rhythmless "fugues" and contrapuntal claptrap, the cooled out solipsism of another middle class, blacks raised up the church, like a funky crucifix held in front of the vampire, and Horace Silver, Art Blakey, Max Roach, Sonny Rollins, and a bunch of other folks used it to create hard bop and funk, to turn the music around again. Because the corporate music doesn't answer black needs, it is the exploiters' theme.

The music is ripped off and then debased for maximum profit. But what is slapped together in this process is a reflection of the white racist oppressor nation, and black people, in the main, reject it. So came the fifties that could experience McCarthyism but still by mid-decade be bursting loose with a Civil Rights movement in the Black Belt, and a hard bop to ready us for Malcolm X and the high level of the black rebellion sixties when John Coltrane would come into his own, to teach us fire music, and then the Ornettes and Shepps, and Aylers and Dolphys and Cecil Taylors, Sun Ra's came, too, carrying the sound and fury of the actual transformation of society.

Where once there had been big band blues played by jazz bands with Kansas City style blues belters, once bebop appeared it seems the big blues bands emerged as separate entities and the rhythm and blues style came into being. The quartet singing style coming out of the late forties is the church again creating a new form in a secular music. The blues continuum develops on its own, as instrumental style, not just as vocal style, and after the big band forties and rhythm and blues, whites have enough access to it to create rock and roll and by the fifties even come over from England jooged not only by Afro-American music but the Caribbean as well with all the calypso and reggae chaps over there. And there is a tendency to revive the styles that blacks have already gone through, as the Dixieland revivalists, or even the modern day restorers of rock and roll.

The apparent "split" in the forties between big band blues and big band (and later small band) jazz is occasioned by the development, most likely, of more distinct class concerns in the black oppressed nation. The avant-garde jazz of the late fifties and early sixties was actually spawned for the first time outside the large black communities, and down in Bohemia. The social structure of an oppressed people is almost completely horizontal but the tiny verticality of the small black middle class as it develops is bound to create a widening contradiction between the black middle class and working class and farmers, so one music goes one way, and the other one quite another. But the existence of rock and roll showed us that now even blues could be seen as an American expression. For the monopoly producers, instant cash from instant hyped-up white teenage bands, a few of which are good, and some that border on minstrelsy.

As the real life fires subsided by the mid-seventies, so, too, did the music seem to have entered into a ditch. Some of the sixties avant-gardists were dead (Trane, Ayler, Dolphy) and some others had gotten so deep into mysticism that their playing continued to be mostly longish OOOMMMs cooled out by metaphysics in replication (though blacker) of one sector of the American petty bourgeoisie. Anytime jazz moves away from the lives of the people, away from the popular expression of the Afro-American majority, which is blues of one form or another, it is literally cooled out and becomes the music of one middle class or another. The best jazz, even when it is expressed by a middle class performer, still reflects the emotional life, the historical reality, of the black masses.

The various kinds of commercial prostitutions and watering downs of the music for monopoly profit are done at the expense of the people—both black people, because they are being exploited economically, culturally, and socially, and other people because they are too often denied the deeper perception of genuinely serious art.

Black people continue to express themselves in spite of, sometimes in reaction to, monopoly music. They cannot be completely melted, their integrity is social and political (their separation) and the aesthetic reflects this.

But the commercialization, "cover," prostitution syndrome is constant. Any new form is reduced, appropriated to be hollowed out, shallowed down and huckstered as soon as it is perceived by the rulers' two-legged antennae (mind bandits). Present-day *fusion* is a restatement of the "cool" tendency that tried to defuse bebop and water it down into elevator music. But black life resists this, hence hard bop and the avant garde. Radio stations like New York's WRVR spew out endless hours of garbage fusion under the disguise of jazz, creating new stars of mediocrity most of whose names will be lost as soon as the fad fades.

The blues-rhythm bottom and cooled-out top is classic exploitation form. (It is a restatement of the American economic system, if you check it!) Insipidity given color, or the old joked-about Cadillac powered not by gas, but when one lifts the hood, a dozen niggers in tennis shoes.

Disco is another perversion of the blues impulse and form. It is a gloss on contemporary urban blues, flattened and vinyled and denutted, so that it can be spread as an endless "environment" and happening, so that the mind can be disconnected and, as Max Roach says, so the powers can "choreograph our ideology." Debrain the flashing body. Disco, like fusion, is commercial music first, and foremost is monopoly music. The four even beats hyped by monster stereo reduces words, all other instruments, sense, and even the reality of place and self to zero. We do not have to know the tune, the performers, or even stop to breathe or reflect. We go on and on and on, bizarre creations of the Board of Directors and our own confusion and cultivated ignorance. We are "cold"—it "can't touch us"—we are high. We freak out. But in frenzied motion, as if we were actually doing something very difficult, accomplishing with our bodies, *disengaged* while seemingly engaged. We are being used.

But real life attacks even hyped-up fantasy. Just as we turn away from happy-go-lucky friendly cops on TV, just in time to see our children murdered by one in the real streets. So the lie of disco commercialism.

Black lives are tortured in reality by the robbery and exploitation of national oppression. Our most beautiful music speaks from within this veil (to paraphrase DuBois) even though it seems to transcend it. The popular music of the sixties (blues) had more progressive lyrics than today when the whole society in economic crisis is being pushed to the right. The sixties upsurge reflected in "Black and Proud," "Respect," "Keep On Pushin'," "Dancin' in the Street," "No Matter How Hard You Try You Can't Stop Me Now," "What's Goin' On," "We're a Winner," has momentarily subsided to the exact extent as the Black Liberation Movement itself. But "The Rich Get Richer," "Get Up Everybody," "Ain't No

Stoppin' Us Now," "Third World Revolution," Stevie Wonder, demonstrate a continuing connection with real life struggle.

Contemporary blues has also evolved a repertory of advanced musical techniques, overdubbing, slick mixing, etc., made rhythmic and harmonic, innovations found in jazz and other musics, in recent years. The fender bass post-Sly is now a lead instrument and this will affect all other musics. The blues line held the popular concern and attention even when jazz had momentarily retreated into metaphysics-land as great musicians like Marvin Gaye, Stevie Wonder, B. B. King, Smokey Robinson, Bobby Blue Bland, the Ojays, continued to develop.

In contemporary jazz is new wealth, but a continuation and extension of the traditional riches of Afro-American music. The World Saxophone Quartet (David Murray, Hammiet Bluiett, Julius Hemphill, Oliver Lake), Black Arthur Blythe, Art Ensemble of Chicago (Lester Bowie, Joseph Jarman, Don Moye, Roscoe Mitchell, Malachi Favors), Air (Steve McCall, Fred Hopkins, Henry Threadgill), Michael Gregory Jackson, Chico Freeman, James Newton, are already astonishing players. They are some of the heirs of the sixties outburst—and there are even, without them, a number of great players still moving and grooving.

Finally, the music is in transition, in this very reactionary period of our society, where the United States is caught between revolution in the Third World and the probability of war with the U.S.S.R.; therefore, they put the weight of their losses and the expenditures for their superweapons onto the backs of the people and the very quality of life in this country is being inferiorized. The Baake decision, opposition to the ERA, reappearance of the Klan and Nazis, restoration of the death penalty, Carter's anti-Iranian jingoism in defense of the Middle Eastern Hitler, the Shah of Iran—all these things are signs of an extreme rightward motion. But black people and the majority of all of us must be strong, facing inflation and recession at the same time, resisting the cutbacks of social programs for B-1 bombers, and neutron bombs; black people must continue to struggle, just as all of us who consider ourselves progressive must continue to struggle, to transform this wretched society. Black music, along with most other things, will reflect those lives and that struggle and the ultimate triumph of the black majority and of the majority of all of us!

[1]H. Bruce Franklin, " 'A' Is for Afro-American: A Primer on the Study of American Literature," *Minnesota Review*, 5 (1975), 53-64.
[2]Amiri Baraka [Leroi Jones] *Blues People: Negro Music in White America*. (New York: W. Morrow Co., 1963; reprinted, Greenwood Press, 1980).

Folk, Popular, Jazz, and Classical Elements in New Orleans

Robert Palmer

AS A PRACTICING CRITIC of popular music and a kind of amateur or ad hoc folklorist, I've noticed that among many folklorists and other academics concerned with American music, rock and roll still seems to be a dirty word (or words). This attitude has been around as long as rock and roll, and implicit in it is the idea that rock and roll is a single, monolithic beast, manufactured solely for profit and the shattering of refined eardrums. I've been involved in researching, teaching, and writing about the early history and pre-history of rock and roll for some years now, and the first point I usually make when addressing a new class or beginning a talk like this one is that rock and roll is not one music but many.

The term "rock and roll," a black slang euphemism for sexual intercourse, was used in the lyrics of "race records" as early as the mid-1920s, and it was a particularly familiar term to the large segment of the American black population that bought and/or listened to rhythm and blues records in the early fifties. (The term "rhythm and blues" meant in the fifties roughly what "race music" meant in the twenties.) The white disc jockey Alan Freed began calling rhythm and blues, or black popular music, "rock and roll" when he launched his celebrated radio show over Cleveland, Ohio's radio station WJW in 1951, and the name stuck. But the rhythm and blues records that were being recorded at that time in Chicago, Memphis, Los Angeles, and New Orleans, to name four important recording centers, had very different characteristics—*regional* characteristics. When the "rock and roll" tag was applied to these musics, and to the black-influenced white music coming out of Memphis, Nashville, Texas, and elsewhere, the various musics didn't lose their regional characteristics. The music was being produced by local entrepreneurs, played by local musicians, and sung by local singers, and although in most cases these people were consciously tailoring their music for an increasingly homogeneous mass audience, especially after rock's sudden burst of popularity in the mid-fifties, not even these commercial considerations eradicated the identifiable and often extremely idiosyncratic regional characteristics the music possessed. Real musical homogenization came later, with the failure of many of the small independent labels that had produced many early rock and roll hits and the increasing centralization of the popular recording industry in New York, Los Angeles, and Nashville. Still, during the sixties and even into the seventies it was still possible to differentiate between, say, a soul record made in Memphis and one made in Chicago, even though most of the artists and musicians came from the same rural roots in the Deep South. The musicians' individual styles were different, the way they functioned as ensembles was different, their sense of rhythm and time were different, and so on. To the extent that localized recording activity still exists in the South, many of these regional differences are still manifest.

Focusing on particular local rock and roll idioms of the fifties, we find that in each case the overall musical and social history of the area played a crucial role in shaping the music and making it special. Folk traditions played a very important part, since most of the first generation of rock and roll musicians came from the lower socioeconomic strata of the community—the same people who tended to preserve traditional rural and urban folklore. The richer an area's musical traditions, the richer the rock and roll produced there.

I've chosen New Orleans as the focus of this lecture because of the exceptional richness of its musical heritage, and especially because of the dialectic between folk, popular, jazz, and classical elements one finds there among both black and white musicians. As it happens, almost all the performers, producers, and songwriters who made rock and roll records in New Orleans during the fifties were black, and they were heirs to an astonishingly diverse set of influences. Back in the eighteenth century when America west of the Mississippi was a wilderness, New Orleans had its own orchestral musicians, trained in France, and was beginning to produce skilled, locally trained classical musicians. The city had its own opera company. The earliest New Orleans jazz musicians, men who matured during the late nineteenth and early twentieth centuries, incorporated operatic arias and light classical melodies into their improvisations, and so did the New Orleans rock and roll musicians of the fifties. Jazz itself exerted a much stronger influence on New Orleans rock and roll than it did on most other regional strains. And, of course, the musicians listened to performers and recordings that were nationally popular.

But perhaps the most important factor of all is that a folk tradition existed in New Orleans, and still does exist there, which is closer to African roots than just about any other folk music in North America. The city was French and Spanish before 1803, and after that date U. S. authorities reluctantly allowed the continuation of what had become a city tradition early on—the Sunday slave gatherings in Congo Square, where blacks danced African-style dances to African-style drumming, often congregating in various corners of the square according to their African tribal affiliations. These slave dances continued right up to the Civil War, and the neo-African music that evolved from them—call and response singing, melodies with a pentatonic cast, polyrhythmic percussion, and perhaps a smattering of African linguistic survivals—has survived among the city's black carnival societies, the so-called Mardi Gras Indians.

I've picked five recordings that will illustrate the richness, diversity, and regional personality of black popular music in New Orleans during the years 1949-58. The first is "Professor Longhair's Blues Rhumba," recorded by Professor Longhair for Atlantic records and reissued on Atlantic 1p SD 7225, *New Orleans Piano*. Longhair was born Henry Roeland Byrd in Bogalusa, Louisiana, in 1918, and grew up mostly in the streets of New Orleans, where he danced for tips on street corners, played orange-crate drums in a children's band, and banged out percussion rhythms as a member of the informal "second line" that cavorted through the streets behind parade bands before teaching himself to play piano on an upright some neighbors had abandoned in an alley. By the time he learned to play piano in his idiosyncratic style, Professor Longhair was well acquainted with New Orleans's folk rhythms. During the 1930s he received further rhythmic education when he joined the Civilian Conservation Corps and found himself working alongside Jamaicans, Cubans, Puerto Ricans, and other people of Caribbean origin, all of whose popular and folk rhythms he studied as carefully as he could. After this experience he "studied" with some of the country-born blues and barrelhouse pianists who frequently played in New Orleans. Out of this combination of influence came a new style that took New Orleans by storm in 1949, when Professor Longhair and his Four Hairs Combo took over a prestigious regular job playing at the Caldonia Inn. The influences are all there in "Professor Longhair's Blues Rhumba." It combines boogie-woogie bass parts and barrelhouse blues figurations in the right hand, more or less conventional r & b saxophone soloing with jazz overtones, and underneath it all, a pure Afro-Cuban clave rhythm, played on a pair of claves. One interesting feature of the record is that the saxophone soloist sounds a little confused by the complexity of the rhythms. Presumably he was a jazz-oriented, "legitimate" or reading musician, like most of the other studio musicians in New Orleans during this period. One of those musicians, saxophonist Red Tyler, has said he found playing with Professor Longhair difficult at first because "his style was unorthodox."

One of the older forms of black American secular folksong, predating the blues, is the narrative ballad, a black variant on the traditional Anglo-American ballad with black protagonists and often a looser narrative structure, usually set in an 8-bar stanza form. The popularity of this nineteenth century form continued in New Orleans well into the rock and roll era, and is evident in numerous recordings. Our next musical example, "Caldonia's Party," was recorded by Smiley Lewis for Imperial in 1953 and most recently reissued on *The Bells are Ringing*, English United Artists UAS 30186. Though he was born and raised in New Orleans, Lewis was heavily influenced by the popular jump blues style that originated in the Southwest during the 1930s and dominated California-recorded r & b after World War II. His vocal style sounds very much like that of the popular Kansas City blues shouter Joe Turner, and on "Caldonia's Party" the pianist plays triplets, a device popularized by Southwestern, California-based pianists like Little Willie Littlefield and Amos Milburn during the early fifties. The song's lyrics are fairly typical of pre-blues folk ballads, but the main character, "Caldonia," was introduced on a popular r & b recording by the former jazz saxophonist Louis Jordan. Even with all these influences, the record has an unmistakable New Orleans flavor, present in the sound of the band, the familiar melody and, especially, some of the lyrics. The last verse—"six months ain't no sentence, and one year ain't no time/They got boys in prison doin' one to ninety-nine"—was a popular one around New Orleans and was usually associated with the Jailbird's blues anthem, "Junker's Blues."

We've already mentioned the Mardi Gras Indians, black

carnival societies that preserve a neo-African or Afro-Caribbean vocal and percussion music. Their traditional songs often revolve around insider's lingo, especially the functions of duties of members of the club or tribe's hierarchy—the king, the queen, the flag boy, the spy boy, and so on. Several Mardi Gras Indian songs that include words in Creole French and, perhaps, some African words, have been recorded more or less verbatim as rock and roll songs. The most commercially successful of these was "Iko Iko," a hit for the Dixie Cups in the early sixties. But "Iko Iko" was based on an earlier recording of the same Mardi Gras theme by a popular New Orleans band of the mid-fifties, Sugar Boy and his Cane Cutters. This version, "Jock-O-Mo," most recently reissued on *Chess Golden Decade Volume One*, English Checker 6445 150, closely follows traditional verses, with its lines about spy boy, flag boy, queen, and king, and alludes to the often bloody battles between rival tribes that took place on Mardi Gras day during the late nineteenth and early twentieth centuries. The words would have been meaningless to listeners outside New Orleans. The record is one of the first of many examples of popular records made in New Orleans using Mardi Gras Indian rhythms, with their pronounced Afro-Caribbean lilt. But notice that when it's time for the obligatory saxophone solo, the rhythm shifts into straight 4/4. Again, the more "legitimately" trained horn players seem to have preferred not to improvise over the rather complex folk rhythm patterns.

Fats Domino, the most popular of all New Orleans rock and roll figures—his record of chart hits in the fifties was exceeded only by Elvis Presley—first recorded in 1949, and his hundreds of sides constitute a fairly complete and very intriguing catalogue of the diverse influences at work in New Orleans's popular music during the fifties and early sixties. Along with his producer, arranger, and musical mastermind Dave Bartholomew, who led the band heard on most New Orleans rock and roll records during the fifties, Domino was an early master of what would today be called "fusion" music. His "When My Dreamboat Comes Home," recorded in 1956 and available on a number of Fats Domino reissues on United Artists and other labels, is an excellent illustration of this fusion process. To begin with, the song comes not from folk tradition or r & b sources but from Tin Pan Alley, from pre-rock and roll popular music. The drumming, by the great Charles "Hungry" Williams, often named as the "inventor" of the "funk" style of drumming, is based on the "second line" rhythm associated with New Orleans's parade bands. Domino's piano playing is influenced by nationally popular jump blues and boogie-woogie pianists, but his singing has a pronounced French lilt that's characteristic of New Orleans—his parents spoke little English. The saxophone solo, one of the instrumental masterpieces of rock and roll, bears repeated listening. Its style suggests the tradition of smooth, flowing, melodic clarinet playing exemplified by New Orleans jazzmen like Jimmie Noone and Sidney Bechet. This manner of playing is a legacy of the Creoles, people of mixed African and European descent who were effectively a third social class in New Orleans, neither officially white nor officially black, until the passage of "Jim Crow" legislation, toward the end of the nineteenth century, forced them to mix more with their black neighbors by segregating them from white society. The Creoles had attained their unusual social position in New Orleans well before the emancipation of the slaves and had provided the city with hundreds of skilled musicians, trained in the European manner. Herb Hardesty's saxophone solo on "When My Dreamboat Comes Home" isn't as hard and bluesy as most of the other saxophone solos heard on rock and roll records in the fifties—it's Creole.

A number of black entertainers have confessed to an early and lasting affection for country and western music, and although this influence was less evident in New Orleans than elsewhere—in many parts of the South, it was the only kind of music other than mainstream white pop that one could hear on the radio— it's very apparent in a 1958 recording of "Little Liza Jane" by Huey "Piano" Smith and the Clowns. This was one of the most popular New Orleans-based rock and roll combos of the late fifties and was known for recordings of novelty material. "Little Liza Jane" is certainly novel for a black New Orleans band; the musicians probably thought of it as country and western hoe-down music, a supposition borne out by the country-style playing and lusty vocal refrains. (The song's actual origins may be in black plantation music.) In the middle of this bit of slightly lunatic black redneck music we find another classic rock and roll tenor saxophone solo, this time by Lee Allen. The solo is built around a fragment of Dvořák's "Humoresque," the fragment being repeated twice in the course of the record as an odd but somehow appropriate thematic thread.

As these five recordings suggest, New Orleans's early rock and roll musicians drew on an intriguingly varied mix of influences, from the classics and country music to neo-African and Afro-Caribbean rhythms, from jazz to nineteenth century ballads. But we could have focused on Memphis or Chicago and come up with a batch of records that illustrated influences that were nearly this diverse. The important point to remember is that rock and roll, like the folk and popular forms from which it sprang, was a true expression of the people who made and supported it. Commercial considerations certainly figured in its creation but these considerations were one factor, and not always a critical one. Sonny Payne, a white Southern disc jockey associated with the King Biscuit Time program that featured bluesman Sonny Boy Williamson, once made a remark about the bluesmen he worked with for so many years that could as easily be applied to rock and roll singers and musicians. "These people are trying to *tell you something,*" he said. "And if you listen long enough and hard enough, you will understand what it's all about." It's important to listen to rock and roll for the same reason it's important to listen to folk music—in order to understand more about our land, our people, and ourselves.

Contributors

Amiri Baraka (Leroi Jones) is a writer, playwright, poet and music critic. Among his works are *Black Music* and *Blues People: Negro Music in White America.*

Doris J. Dyen, an ethnomusicologist, is editor and writer at the Florida Folklife Program. She is coauthor of the article on North American folk music in the *New Grove Dictionary of Music and Musicians,* and an editor of the recently published *Resources of American Music History.*

Dena J. Epstein is assistant music librarian at the University of Chicago and the author of *Sinful Tunes and Spirituals: Black Folk Music to the Civil War* and *Music Publishing in Chicago Before the Fire.*

David Evans, the author of *Tommy Johnson* and *Big Road Blues,* is associate professor of music and director of regional studies in ethnomusicology at Memphis State University.

William Ferris, director of the Center for the Study of Southern Culture and professor of anthropology at the University of Mississippi, is the author of *Blues from the Delta.*

Kenneth S. Goldstein is professor of folklore and folklife at the University of Pennsylvania and author of *A Guide for Field Workers in Folklore* and *Two Penny Ballads and Four Dollar Whiskey.*

Anthony Heilbut, music historian and record producer, has written *The Gospel Sound: Good News and Bad Times* and has received both the Grand Prix du Disque and the Grammy award. His study of artistic and intellectual emigrés from Hitler will be published later this year by Viking Press.

William Ivey, is director of the Country Music Foundation, Nashville, Tennessee, as well as a trustee of the National Academy of Recording Arts and Sciences.

Charles Keil, associate professor of American Studies at the State University of New York at Buffalo, is the author of *Urban Blues* and *Tiv Song*.

A. L. Lloyd, music critic and historian, serves on the European Permanent Commission for the Study of Industrial Folklore and on the International Folk Music Council. Among his contributions to the study of folk music are *Folk Song in England* and *Folk Songs of the Americas*.

Bill C. Malone is associate professor of history at Tulane University. He is the author of *Country Music U.S.A.* and *Southern Music/American Music*. The coeditor of *Stars of Country Music*, he recently edited the recorded anthology *The Smithsonian Collection of Classic Country Music*.

Robert Palmer is music critic for the *New York Times* and a contributing editor to *Rolling Stone*. He has published *Baby, That Was Rock and Roll; A Tale of Two Cities: Memphis Rock and New Orleans Roll* and, most recently, *Deep Blues*.

Vivian Perlis lectures in American Studies and is research associate in the School of Music at Yale University. The director of the American Music Oral History Project, she is the author of *Charles Ives Remembered*.

Mark Slobin is associate professor of music at Wesleyan University, Middletown, Connecticut. He is the author of *Kirgiz Instrumental Music* and *Music in the Culture of Northern Afghanistan* and of two forthcoming works, *Tenement Songs: The Popular Music of the Jewish Immi-*

grant (University of Illinois Press) and *Old Jewish Folk Songs and Fiddle Tunes: The Writings and Collections of Moshe Beregovski* (University of Pennsylvania Press).

Richard Spottswood edited the Ethnic Musical Heritage Series for the American Folklife Center at the Library of Congress and is the author of *Ethnic Music on Records, 1895-1942.*

Charles K. Wolfe is associate professor of English at Middle Tennessee State University. He has edited Alton Delmore's autobiography *Truth Is Stranger Than Publicity* and, in addition, is the author of *Grand Ole Opry: The Early Years; Riley Puckett;* and *Tennessee Strings: The Story of Country Music in Tennessee.*

Index

Abernathy, Lee Roy, 87, 88-9, 90, 93, 97-8
Acuff, Roy, 121, 124
Afro-American Folk Songs, 156
Afro-Caribbean music, 189, 197, 199, 201
Ailey, Alvin, 102
"Ain't No Stoppin' Us Now," 191
Air (jazz group), 192
Alabama, Sacred Harp singing in, 74, 75, 76
Aleichem, Sholom, 29
Allen, Lee, 201
All-night singings, 90-6, 97
Almanac Singers, viii
"Amapola," 64
Amato, Gennaro, 65
"Amazing Grace," 96, 102
Ampolaires, 43
Anderson, John, 127
Anderson, Robert, 110
Andrews, Inez, 109
Andrews Sisters, 29, 89
Anglo-American Folksong Scholarship Since 1898 (Wilgus), 153
Anita Kerr Singers, 80
Archive of American Folk Song (Library of Congress), vii, ix, 104

Arnaz, Desi, 64
Arnold, Eddy, 54, 92, 123, 132, 133
Art Ensemble of Chicago, 192
Asch, Moses, viii
ATCO Quartet, 88
Atkins, Chet, 132-3
Autry, Gene, 54
Ayler, Albert, 189, 190

"Back Home Again," 138
Baez, Joan, viii, 134
Bailes Brothers, 80
Ballads, 130, 166, 179, 198
Baltz, George, 36
Bandy, Moe, 127, 128n
Baring-Gould, Sabine, 5
"Barney Google," 67
Barry Sisters, 29
Bartholomew, Dave, 199
Bashell, Louis, 36, 49-55
Basie, Count, 48, 188
Baxter, J. R., Jr., 87
"Bay mir bist du sheyn," 28
B. F. White Sacred Harp (Cooper, 1902), 74, 75-6
The Beatles, 170
Bebop, 167, 188, 189
Bechet, Sidney, 200
"Beer Barrel Polka," 68
Beiderbecke, Bix, 55

The Bells Are Ringing (recording), 198
"Bel mir bist du schoen," 70
Bennett, Tony, 135
Benton, Brook, 111
Berlin, Irving, 26
Bernard, Al, 168
Berry, Chuck, 111, 169, 170
Bevsek, Frankie, 36
Beyer, Tony, 40
Big bands, 183, 188, 189
"Big John," 136
Big Steve (polka band), 34
Birmingham Jubilee Singers, 105
Birmingham Quartet, 167
"Black and Proud," 191
Black music: influence on American music, xiii, 45, 48, 177; development of, xiii, 130, 183-4, 192; commercial exploitation of, xiii, 187-8, 190-1. *See also* Blues; Boogie woogie; Jazz; Gospel music; Sacred Harp; Spirituals (black); Ragtime; Rhythm and blues; Rock and roll; Soul music.
Blackwood Brothers, 80, 84, 86, 87, 95, 98, 99
Blakey, Art, 188
Bland, Bobby "Blue", 47, 171, 192
Blazonczyk, Eddie, 43, 48, 51, 61, 70
Bluegrass, 124, 127, 135, 138
Blues: influence on American music, xiii, 87, 107, 108, 110, 115, 163-76, 190-1, 197, 198, 200; history, development of, 45, 46, 47, 111, 130, 170-1, 177-8, 179-80, 182-3, 189, 201; recording of, 46, 66, 67, 103; instrumentation in, 165, 189, 192
"Blue Skirt Waltz," 34, 36, 40, 42, 52
Bluiett, Hammiet, 192

Blythe, Black Arthur, 192
Bo Diddley, 169
Boogie woogie, 89, 197, 200
"Boogie Woogie," 89
"Boogie Woogie Bugle Boy," 89
Book of American Negro Spirituals (Johnson), 156
Boone, Pat, 90
"Born to Lose," 121
"Borrowed Angel," 128
"The Bottle Let Me Down," 126
Bowie, Lester, 192
Boxcar Willie, 127
Bradford, Alex, 115
Bradley, Owen, 132
Brewster, (Rev.) W. Herbert, 107, 109, 111, 112, 113, 115
Brice, Fannie, 28, 29
Broadwood, Lucy, 5
Bronson, B. H., 8
Brown, James, 111, 171
Brown, Lois, 173
Brown, Milton, 169
Brumley, Albert E., 87, 93
Bruner, Cliff, 121
Burnette, Ranie, 175
Burnside, R. L., 174, 175
Bush, Johnny, 125

Cahill, Marie, 168
Cajun music, 61, 168
"Caldonia's Party," 198
Campbell, Glen, 122
Campbell, Lucie E., 106
"Cam Ye O're frae France?," 17
Canned Heat (band), 170
The Caravans, 111
Carlisle, Cliff, 92
Carr, Wynona, 110
Carson, Martha, 80, 92, 98, 99
Charles, Ray, 109, 111, 112
Cheeks, (Rev.) Julius, 112
Chenier, Clifton, 70
Cherokee Cowboys, 125
Chess Golden Decade Volume One (recording), 199

Index 207

Chuck Wagon Boys, 80, 83, 95
Civil Rights Movement, viii, 109, 112, 171, 188
"Clarinet Polka," 70
Classical music, 168
Cleveland, James, 112
Cline, Patsy, 132, 133
Coates, Dorothy Love, 104
Cohan, George M., 26
Coleman, Ornette, 189
Colored Sacred Harp (Jackson), 76, 77
Coltrane, John, 186, 189, 190
The Consolers, 106
Cooke, Sam, 111
Cooper, W. M., 74, 75-6
Copland, Aaron, 186
Copper family, 10
"Corn Licker Still in Georgia," 66
Country music: honky tonk style, xii, 119-28, 138, 169; recording of, 60, 66, 67; development of, 80-1, 84, 103, 168-9; instrumentation in, 122-3, 124, 125; Outlaw Movement, 138; influence on rock and roll, 169, 200-1; mentioned, 54, 57, 108. *See also* Nashville Sound.
Cousin Fuzzy (polka band), 41
Cox, Harry, 9
Crain, Silas Roy, 108
Cravens, Rupert, 96-7
"Crazy Arms," 125, 128n
Crosby, Bing, 92
"Crossing over Jordan," 93
Crouch, Andrae, 115
Cuarteto Coculense, 64
"La Cucaracha," 64, 70
Cugat, Xavier, 64

Daffan, Ted, 121
"Dancin' in the Street," 191
Daniel, John, 82, 91-2
Daniels, (Rev.) W. Leo, 104

David's Violin (Davids fidele), 23, 24
Davis Sisters, 110, 112
"The Day Is Past and Gone," 102
"Dead Cat on the Line," 103
Dean, Jimmie, 136
Demetriades, Tetos, 69
Denny, Sandy, 16
Denson, Paine, 74, 75, 76, 79
Denver, John, 138
"Dese Bones a Gwinna Rise Agin," 93
Dexter, Al, 121
Diamond, Neil, 30
Disco, xiii, 113, 191
Dixie Cups, 199
Dixie Hummingbirds, 108, 110, 111
Dolphy, Eric, 189, 190
Domino, Fats, 111, 169, 199-200
Donegan, Lonnie, 5
"Don't Be Cruel," 64
"Don't Worry," 136
Dorsey, Thomas A., 103, 106-7, 115, 168
Dranes, Arizona, 105
Duchow, Lawrence, 40, 52
Dvorak, Anton, 201
Dylan, Bob, viii, 30, 115, 134, 170

Edwards, Cliff, 168
Edwards, Stoney, 128n
Edwin Hawkins Singers, 113
Ellington, Duke, 48, 184, 186, 188
Ellis, Vep, 87
Ellstein, Abraham (Leon Stenier), 28, 30, 68
Emerson, Ralph Waldo, 145, 147, 148
Emmons, Buddy, 125
Estes, Milton, 92
Ethnic music, recording of in

U.S., xi, 60-70
Ethnomusicologist (Hood), 153

Fairfield Four, 112
Fairport Convention Band, 16, 18
Famous Blue Jay Singers, 107
Favors, Malachi, 192
Fiddler on the Roof, sources of, xi, 21-31
Fieldstones, 173
First Symphony (Ives), 143
Fitzgerald, Ella, 113
Five Blind Boys, 110
Five Hand Reel, 18
"The Florida Storm," 106
Foley, Red, 90
Folk Culture on St. Helena Island, South Carolina (Johnson), 158
Folk music, American: scholarship on, vii-xiv; revival, vii, 169; evolution into new forms, x, 21, 22, 57, 195-6; impact of technology on, 46-7, 73-5, 76, 79, 130; Afro-American, 151-61
Folk music, British: revival, 3-13, 14-18; impact of technology on, 3-13, 14, 15-18
Folk Music in America (recording series), xi, 60, 67
Fowler, Wally, 86, 87, 90, 91, 92-6
Franklin, Aretha, 113, 171
Franklin, C. L. (Rev.), 104
Freed, Alan, 194
Freeman, Chico, 192
Fritz the Plumber (polka band), 35
Frizzell, Lefty, 123, 127
Fusion music, 190, 191, 199-200

Gale, Bill (Wasyl Gula), 68
Garcia, Ramon, 64
Gates, (Rev.) J.M., 103-4
"Gavotte" (*Shir hashirim*), 25
Gaye, Marvin, 192
Gentleman Jim (polka band leader), 51
Georgia Clodhoppers, 92
Gershwin, George, 168, 186
"Get Up Everybody," 191
Gibson, Don, 133
"Girl from Impanema," 64
Glahe, Will, 68
Golden Gate Jubilee Quartet, 108, 109
Goldfadn, Abraham, 22-3, 27, 29
Goldstein, Morris, 65
Goodman family, 95
Gordon, Robert W., 156
Gorgaza, Emilio de, 64
Gospel All Stars, 112
"Gospel Boogie," 88-90
Gospel music, black: commercialization of, xii, 80, 101-15; influences on American music, xii, 87, 98, 111, 112, 113, 114; influences on, 103-4, 106, 115, 168
Gospel music, white: commercialization of, xi-xii, 80-100; influences on, 85-6, 98, 106
Gosz, Romy, 41, 55
Grand Ole Opry, 82, 91, 92, 122
"The Grand Tour," 128
Great Britain, folk music revival in, 3-13, 14-18
Green, Al, 113
Green, Lil, 108
Griffin, Rex, 121
Guthrie, Woody, viii

Haggard, Merle, 126
Haley, Bill, 169
Hall, Connor, 88, 89, 90, 96
"Hallelujah, I Love Her So," 112
Hamblen, Stuart, 98
Hammond, John, 115
Handy, W. C., 107, 166

Index

Hardesty, Herb, 200
Harmoneers, 80
Harmonizing Four, 109
"Harper Valley PTA," 136
Harpo, Slim, 170
Harris, Marion, 168
Harris, R. H., 108, 111
"Hava Nagila," 30
Hawaiian music, 168
"Help Me Make It Through the Night," 138
Hemphill, Jessie Mae, 173, 175
Hemphill, Julius, 192
Henderson, Fletcher, 187, 188
"He Touched Me," 106
"Hey, Cavalier," 52
"Hide Me in Thy Bosom," 107
Hill, Jessie May, 105
Hill, Raymond, 174
Hoffman, Johnny, 52
"Hold to God's Unchanging Hand," 106
"Der holekh ve dor bo," 23, 24
Holiday, Billie, 113, 186
Holiday Quickstep, 142
Holmes, Jimmy, 173-4
Homeland Harmony Quartet, xi, 88, 89, 90, 91, 95
Honky tonk, defined, 128 n
"Honky Tonk Blues," 128 n
Hood, Mantle, 153
Hooker, John Lee, 170, 171
Hopkins, Fred, 192
Hopkins, Lightnin', 170
Hornbostel, Erich von, 156
Hot Five, 186
House, Eddie "Son", 170
"How I Got Over," 111
Howlin' Wolf, 170
Hudman, Clara, 104, 105
Hughes, Langston, 183
Humeniuk, Pawlo (Paul), 66
"Humoresque," 201
Hurt, Mississippi John, 170, 174
Hyles, Arnold, 91

"I Don't Feel No Ways Tired,"

"Ikh zing" ("I Sing"), 28
"Iko Iko," 199
"I'll Fly Away," 106
"I'll Overcome," 106
"I'm a Short Fat Mama," 108
"I'm Climbing Higher and Higher," 109
Instrumentation: in polka, 35, 37, 38, 44-5, 46, 48, 52, 57; in black gospel, 105; in honky tonk country, 122-3, 124, 125, 127-8; in the Nashville Sound, 130, 132, 134, 135, 136, 137; in blues, 165, 168, 182, 189, 192; in jazz, 182; in New Orleans rock and roll, 197-8, 199, 200, 201
Isley Brothers, 111
"Israel, " 29
"It Makes No Difference Now," 121
"It Must Be Jesus," 111
"It's Tight Like That," 103
Iturbi, Jose, 64
"It Was Always So Easy (To Find an Unhappy Woman)," 128n
"I've Got a New Home," 111
"I've Got a Woman," 111
Ives, Charles, xii, 141-50, 186
"I Write the Songs," 112

Jackson, George Pullen, 158-9, 160
Jackson, Judge, 76
Jackson, Mahalia, 107, 109, 111, 113, 115
Jackson, Michael, 113
Jackson, Michael Gregory, 192
Jackson, ("Aunt") Molly, viii
Jackson, Otis, 109
Jackson, Tommy, 125
James, "Skip", 174
James, Sonny, 133

Jarman, Joseph, 192
Jaworski, Walt, 34
Jazz: development of, xiii, 84, 101, 106, 177, 178, 182, 184, 189, 190, 192; influence on American music, 55, 87, 196, 197, 201; influences on, 105, 167; mentioned, ix, 43, 67, 110
"Jealous Heart," 54
Jefferson, Blind Lemon, 167
"Jelly Roll Blues," 105
"Jesus Hits Like an Atom Bomb," 87
Jeter, (Rev.) Claude, 113
"Jock-O-Mo," 199
John Edwards Memorial Foundation (UCLA), ix
Johnnie and Jack, 92
John, Olivia Newton, 138
Johnson, Bessie, 105
Johnson, Guy Benton, 158
Johnson, James Weldon, 156
Johnson, Robert, 130
Johnson Sisters, 95
Johnson, ("Blind") Willie, 105-6, 168
Jolly Polecats, 36
Jolson, Al, 28, 29
Jones, George, 125, 128
Jones, (Rev.) Johnny L., 104
Jordan, Louis, 198
Jordanaires, 98
Jordon, Fred, 9
Jubilee Songs, 159
Juju (Yoruba), 45, 46
"Junker's Blues," 198
"Just a Closer Walk with Thee," 110
"Just Because," 35, 40, 52

Karpek, George, 37
Kay, Dolly, 168
"Keep On Pushin'," 191
Kidson, Frank, 5
Kincaid, Bradley, 62

King, Albert, 171
King, B. B., 47, 58, 111, 171, 192
Kirkpatrick, John, 144
Knight, Marie, 110
Kol Nidre, 30
Krehbiel, Henry, 156
Krupa, Gene, 55

Laine, Frankie, 112
Lake, Oliver, 192
Landford, Bill, 108
Larner, Sam, 9
"The Last Letter," 121
Lateiner, Joseph, 23
Law, Don, 132, 133
Ledbetter, Huddie "Leadbelly", viii
Lee, Brenda, 133
LeFevre Trio, 80
"Let Jesus Fix It for You," 106
"Let's All Be Americans Now," 26
Lewis, Jerry Lee, 126, 169
Lewis, Smiley, 198
"Life Is Like A Mountain Railroad," 106
Lil' Wally, 34, 41
"Lincoln, The Great Commoner," 149
Lister, Hovie, 88, 89
Lister, Mosie, 87, 89
Littlefield, "Little Willie", 198
"Little Liza Jane," 201
Little Milton, 171
Little Richard, 111, 169
"Lonely Avenue," 111
Longhair, Professor, 197-8
"The Lord's Prayer," 111
Louvin Brothers, 80
"Lovely on the Water," 17-18
"The Love of God," 112
Lunceford, Jimmy, 188
Lush, Marion, 48, 52, 61
Lynn, Loretta, 126
Lyrics, themes of: in British

Index

folk bands' repertoire, 17; in blues, 165-6, 167; in country music, 119, 121, 128
McCall, Steve, 192
McCollum, Mother, 105
McCoy, James, 88
McCoy, Otis, 88
McCrary, (Rev.) Sam, 112
MacDonald Brothers Quarter, 82, 83
McGhee, Brownie, 170
McKay, Claude, 183
McPhatter, Clyde, 109
Madden, Sammy, 52
"The Majority," 149
Mamale, 28
"El Manicero" ("The Peanut Vendor"), 64
Mardi Gras Indians, 197, 198-9
Martin, Leroy, 173
Martin, Roberta, 104, 107, 110
Martin, Sallie, 107, 108, 115
Martinsek, Tony, 49, 53
Mattey, Irv, 35
Maupin, Jimmy, 34-41
Max and the Merrymakers, 34, 35
May, ("Brother") Joe, 115
"Mayne zeydes nign" ("Grandpa's Tune"), 27
Mendoza, Lydia, 70
Milburn, Amos, 198
Miller, Roger, 125
Milsap, Ronnie, 126
Milwaukee, polka style in, xi, 32-58
Mitchell, Roscoe, 192
"Mr. Gallagher and Mr. Shean," 67, 70
Modern Mountaineers, 88
Mogulesco, Sigmund, 23, 25
"Mon homme" ("My Man"), 28
"Moonlight and Roses," 54
"Mother's Prayer," 92
"Move on Up a Little Higher," 111
Moye, Don, 192
Mullican, Moon, 121

Murray, Anne, 130
Murray, David, 192

Narmour (Willie) and Smith (Shell), 62
Nashville Sound: commercialization and tradition in, xii, 124, 126, 129-38; instrumentation in, 133, 134-5, 138
Nelson, Willie, 125
"Never Ending Love," 54
"Never Grow Old," 106
New Orleans, early rock and roll in, xiii, 194-201
New Orleans Piano (recording), 197
"The New River," 149
Newton, James, 192
New Yorkers, 34
"No Matter How Hard You Try You Can't Stop Me Now," 191
Noone, Jimmie, 200
Norfolk Jubilee Singers (Norfolk Jazz Quartet), 105, 107, 167
Norteño music, 61, 64

Oak Ridge Quartet, 92, 93, 95, 99
O'Connor, George, 168
O'Daniel, W. Lee, 169
"O Happy Day," 113
The Ojays, 192
"Old Hank and Lefty Raised My Country Soul," 128n
Old Hickory Singers, 82
Old-time music, 138
Olinski, Eddie, 34
Olshanetsky, Alexander, 28
"Onkl Sem," ("Uncle Sam"), 26
Original Gospel Harmonettes, 110
Original Sacred Harp (Denson, 1936), 74
Owens, Buck, 125
Owens, Henry, 108
Owens, Jack, 174

Oxford, Vernon, 127

"Paddy's Green Shamrock Shore," 18
Pardon, Walter, 9, 11, 17
Parker, Charlie, 186
"Pass Me By," 126
Paycheck, Johnny, 125
"Peanut Polka," 40
Pecon, Johnny, 41
Pegg, Bob, 12
Perkins, Carl, 169
Pickett, Wilson, 112, 171
Picon, Molly, 27-8
Pierce, Webb, 122, 123
Pilgrim Travelers, 90, 110, 111
Pinchik, Pierre, 62
"Pistol Packin' Mama, " 121
Plantation Melodies (Christy), 154
Polka, Slovenian style in Milwaukee, xi, 35-58
Pop music, 15, 23, 84, 85, 87, 99, 113, 114, 132, 134, 137, 200
"Pray, Pray, Pray for the U.S.A.," 87, 93
Preachers and black gospel style, 103-4
"Precious Memories," 106
Presley, Elvis, 112, 124, 169, 199
Price, Ray, 125, 128n
Price, Sammy, 112
Primitive Music (Wallaschek), 153, 155
Prior, Maddy, 16
Prodo, Perez, 64
"Professor Longhair's Blues Rhumba," 197
"Propaganda Papa," 92
Pugel, Rudy, 36
Pugh, Brother and Sister, 106

Quartets: white gospel, 80-100; black gospel, 104-5, 106, 108, 109, 110, 166, 167

Ragtime, 165, 166, 167
"Raindrops Keep Falling on My Head," 29
"Ramona," 67
The Rangers, 83, 86, 88, 91, 95
Reagan, Bernice, viii
Rebetika (Greek), 45, 46
Recording: of ethnic music in the U.S., xi, 60-70; and British folksong revival, 6-13; and Sacred Harp traditions, 74, 75, 79; of gospel music, 85-6, 110
Redding, Otis, 111
Reed, Jimmy, 169
Reed, Lula, 110
Reeves, Jim, 132, 133
"Respect," 191
"Respect Yourself," 113
"Reynardine," 16
Rhythm and blues, 105, 110, 112, 189, 194, 195, 197, 198
"The Rich Get Richer," 191
"Rich Young Ruler," 88
"Riding the Range for Jesus," 87
"Rise Again," 106
Roach, Max, 188, 191
Robbins, Marty, 132, 133, 136
Robertson, Jeannie, 9
Robeson, Paul, 109
Robinson, B. C., 88
Robinson, Smokey, 192
Rock and roll: in New Orleans, xiii, 194-201; impact on American musical world, 123, 124, 131; musical influences on, 111, 124, 169, 170, 189, 196-7, 201; mentioned, 110, 114, 125
"Rock Me," 107
Rodgers, Dick, 36
Rodgers, Jimmie, viii, 60, 168
Rodriguez, Johnny, 126
Rogers, Kenny, 130
Rolling Stones, 170
Rollins, Sonny, 188
"Romance in the Dark," 108

Ronstadt, Linda, 138
Rosenblatt, Joseph, 62
"Rum and Coca-Cola," 70
Rumshinsky, Joseph, 24-5, 28
Rupp, Art, 108

Sacred Harp: changes in traditions, xi, 73-9; black singers of, 75-9
Sacred Harp (B. F. White, 1869), 74
Salinas, Beto, 40
Sandburg, Carl, vii
Schwartz, Abe, 62
"Second Hand Rose of Second Avenue," 28
Secunda, Sholom, 28
Seeger, Charles, vii
Seeger, Pete, viii
Sharp, Cecil, 5
Sharpe, Claude, 82
Shaw, ("Sister") Rosa, 109
Shea, George Beverly, 80, 99
Shepp, Archie, 189
Shir hashirim (Song of Songs), 25
"Shout," 111
"Silk Umbrella Polka," 49
Silver, Horace, 188
Simon, Paul, 115
Sinatra, Frank, 92, 135
Singing conventions, xii, 82, 86, 96, 97, 99
Singing schools, 75, 82, 93
Six Fat Dutchmen, 52
Skillet Lickers, 60, 66
"Skipping Around," 128n
Skrathult, Olle I, 65
Slavery, xiii, 177, 178
Slave Songs of the United States, 154, 155
"Slowly," 122
Smith, Bessie, 60, 107, 186
Smith, Huey "Piano", 201
Smith, Lucius, 166
Smith, Mayne, 135
Smith, "Pinetop", 89
Smith, Sammi, 138

Smith, Willie Mae Ford, 107, 115
Smith's Sacred Singers, 85
Solek, Walt, 34, 51
Soul music, 103, 111, 112, 113, 171, 195
Southerners, migration, urbanization of, xii, 120, 127, 183
Southern Tones, 111
Speer Family, 82, 95
Spicher, Buddy, 125
Spirituals (black), xii-xiii, 152-60, 155-7, 159, 160, 165, 179
"Stalin Wasn't Stalling," 109
Stamps-Baxter Company, 81, 82, 83, 84, 87, 88, 91, 93
Stamps, Frank, 84, 94, 98
Stamps, V. O., 84
"Stand By Me," 106
Staples, Mavis, 113
Staples Singers, 113, 168
"Stardust," 64
Starr, Kay, 112
"Star-Spangled Banner," 26
The Statesmen, 86, 87, 88, 95, 96, 99
Steeleye Span (electric folk band), 16, 17, 18
Stevens, (Prof.) Herman, 111
Stewart, Belle, 9
Stewart, Rod, 187
Stewart, Wynn, 125
"Stormy Weather," 108
"The Storm Is Passing Over," 106
Streisand, Barbra, 135
Strickland, Napoleon, 175
String band music, 130
"Strut Miss Lizzie," 105
Stuckey, Henry, 174
Studio musicians: and the Nashville Sound, 133-4, 136-7; and New Orleans rock and roll, 198
Sugar Boy and His Cane Cutters, 199
Summer, Donna, 113

Sun Ra, 189
The Supremes, 171
"Sure Do Need Him Now," 109
"Surely God Is Able (To Carry You Through)," 109
Swan Silvertones, 113
Swarbrick, Dave, 16
"Sweethearts on Parade," 54
"Swinging Doors," 126

"Take Your Burdens to the Lord," 106
Tallmadge, William, 76
Tanner, Phil, 9
Tape recorder, and Britain's folk song revival, 6-13
Tawney, Cyril, 12
Taylor, Cecil, 189
Taylor, Johnny, 112
"Tea for Two," 29
Technology, impact on folk music, x, 3-13, 14, 15-16, 18, 46-7, 66, 82, 122-3, 125, 130
"Tell Me Why," 110
Terley, Eddie (Edmund Terlikowski), 68
Terry, Sonny, 170
Teschmaker, Frank, 55
Tharpe, ("Sister") Rosetta, xii, 90, 107, 108, 112, 115, 168
"That's How Much I Love You," 92
"That's Why I Love Him So, " 112
"There's a Tree on Each Side of the River," 112
"Third World Revolution," 192
"This Little Girl of Mine," 111
Thompson, Hank, 123
Thoreau, David, vii, 145, 148
Threadgill, Henry, 192
Tillman, Floyd, 121, 123, 128n
Tindley, C. A., 106
The Treltones, 57
Trolli, Joe, 41

Tubb, Ernest, 122, 124, 125, 126, 127, 128n
Tucker, Ira, 111
Tucker, Sophie, 168
Tulane Jazz Archives (New Orleans), ix
Turner, Andrew, 174
Turner, Ike, 174
Turner, ("Big") Joe, 169, 198
"Turn Your Radio On," 96
Two Gospel Keys, 109
"Two Little Flowers," 146
Tyler, Red, 198

Ubick (Chet) and the Ubick Brothers, 36
"Ukrainian Wedding," 66
Ulatowski, Ignacy, 65

Valdez, Miguelito, 64
Variations on America, 145
Vaughan (James D.) Company, 81, 82, 84, 94, 99
Vaughan Williams, Ralph, 17
Verdell, Jacqui, 113
"Vote for Names, Names, with Teddy, Woodrow and Bill," 147
"Vox zol ikh tun az. . ." (What Can I Do? I Love Him"), 28

Wade, Norman, 127
Waits, Jim, 91
Walbert, James D., 94
Walker, Charlie, 125
"Walking the Floor Over You," 128n
Wallaschek, Richard, 153, 154, 155
Walters, Johnny, 52
Ward, Clara, 107, 110, 113, 115
Washington, Dinah, 108-9
Waters, Muddy, 170, 171
The Watersons, 10
Watkins, Charles, 110
Watson, Gene, 127
Watts, Isaac, 102, 107, 114

The Weavers, viii
"Weeping May Endure for a Night," 107
Welk, Lawrence, 37
"We'll Understand It Better By and By," 106
"We're a Winner," 191
"We Shall Overcome," viii, 106
Western swing, 123, 138
Wettling, George, 55
"What Kind of Man Is This," 111
"What's Goin' On," 191
"When I Take My Vacation in Heaven," 106
"When My Dreamboat Comes Home," 200
"When the Fire Comes Down," 93
"When the Saints Go Marching In," 96, 111
White, Benjamin Franklin, 74
White, Newman Ivey, 156
White and Negro Spirituals (Jackson), 159
White Spirituals in the Southern Uplands (Jackson), 158-9
Whitman, Walt, vii, 143
"Who'll Turn Out the Lights?," 128
"Who's Making Love to Your Old Lady While You're Out Making Love?," 104
Wilfahrt, ("Whoopee") John, 62
Wilgus, D. K., 4, 153, 156
"Will the Circle Be Unbroken," 106
Williams, Charles "Hungry", 200
Williams, Dewey P., 78
Williams, Hank, xii, 119, 123-4, 125, 127, 169
Williams Hank, Jr., 126
Williams, J. Mayo, 167
Williams, ("Big") Joe, 170, 175
Williams, Marion, 107, 109, 111, 113
Williamson, Sonny Boy, 201

Wills, Bob, 121, 169
Wilson, Jackie, 111
Winkler, David Paul (D. P.), 42-4, 45, 48-9
Wiregrass Sacred Harp Singers, xi, 77-9
Wisniewski, Gene, 34
Wonder, Stevie, 113, 130, 192
"Wonderful Time Up There," 90
Wood, Randy, 90
Worksongs, 165, 179
World Saxophone Quartet, 192
Wright, Eugene, 87

"Yanke Dudil in G," 26
Yankovic, Frankie, xi, 34-5, 36, 37-9, 40, 41-2, 43-4, 45-6, 47-8, 49, 50, 51-2, 56, 57, 58
The Yardbirds, 170
"Yellow Rose of Texas," 154
"Yes, We Have No Bananas," 67
Yiddish-American theater, xi, 21, 22-5
YIVO Institute for Jewish Research (New York), ix, 26
Young, Margaret, 168
The Young Tradition (folk singers), 10
"Your Cheatin' Heart," 54
"You're a Grand Old Flag," 26
"You're the Best Thing That Ever Happened to Me," 112

Zuckerberg, Regina, 25, 27
Zurawaki, John, 43

www.ingramcontent.com/pod-product-compliance
Lightning Source LLC
Chambersburg PA
CBHW030342240426
43661CB00052B/1719